AUTUMN RHYTHM

AUTUMN
RHYTHM

RICHARD MELTZER

Musings on Time, Tide,
Aging, Dying, and Such Biz

DA CAPO PRESS
A Member of the Perseus Books Group

Cataloging-in-Publication data for this book is available from the Library of Congress

Design by Jeff Williams
Set in 11-point Berling by the Perseus Books Group

ISBN 0-306-81228-2
Published by Da Capo Press
A Member of the Perseus Books Group
http://www.dacapopress.com

Da Capo Press books are available at special discounts for bulk purchases in the U.S. by corporations, institutions, and other organizations. For more information, please contact the Special Markets Department at the Perseus Books Group, 11 Cambridge Center, Cambridge, MA 02142, or call (800) 255-1514 or (617) 252-5298, or e-mail j.mccrary@perseusbooks.com.

1 2 3 4 5 6 7 8 9—07 06 05 04 03

To Malcolm Cross, to Hopper, and to
all my friends who got me through,
well, you know what . . .

TABLE OF CONTENTS

INTRODUCTION

I . . . I . . . I . . . I . . . I, I, I, I.
—"Two Tub Man," the Dictators

Well, here we are—and where the hell is THAT?

In the intro to my last book, I wore the endgame face of a geezer, an oldguy, speculating that it might in fact be my *final book*. I was joking, natch, and I'd also probably been listening to Robert Johnson—my time, like his, didn't *appear* 'specially long—but mainly (I think) it just didn't feel so homey, so hot, living in my own skin back then. Y'never know how these things are gonna play out, eh?—'cause now I feel kinda like I've found that home. It may be held together with large volumes of spit, and subject to change without high-sign or premonition, but this week, anyway, it feels rooty toot.

An interesting outcome, wouldn't you say?—not the longest of longshots, but unlikely nonetheless: that what we have here would be a sequel-of-sorts not to the book that followed that intro, but to the intro itself: an actual "geezer book," or some such . . . hey hey.

In the same introduction, I worried all too loud and sweaty 'bout being typecast, make that re-typecast, as a rockwriter. If I were the worrying "kind," I could be fretting now about being cast as a deathanddyingwriter . . . haw . . . thank fuck I am *not* that kind. I don't fuss & fidget over FRAMES getting drawn around what-all it is I feel motivated to do, writewise, anymore . . . I just *do*.

(For the record: rock-crit *is* often what mags ask of me nowadays . . . ask, but don't always get . . . but I'll live, y'know?)

About 10 years ago, I had this agent whose bright idea it was to turn me into "the new Charles Bukowski"—as if being such a creature would render me the heppest in writeperson merchandise. The old Bukowski had died, see, and my agent-man saw the world clamoring for a replacement. If we could only scare up some token resemblance between Buk and myself, he insisted, we could parlay that into a calling card that would last me all the days of my life. To pull it off, I'd've had to at least be and behave like an "old curmudgeon" . . . oboy . . . well let's just say I didn't go for the bait. (Imagine if I'd let THAT be my lot, my casting . . . pretty scary, huh?)

"A Stiff for All Seasons," my kiss-off of the curmudgeon himself, is the final prose piece here, as well as the oldest, written in '97. The two most recent, my title piece and "Middle Beginning End," may be handier in giving you a sense of who "I" am, and where I currently am "at"—in real time, in write time—which brings us to the "topic" at hand: your time

. . . my time . . . all our times running low, running out, or in any case *running*.

When I was 28 or 29—inotherwords, HALF MY LIFE ago—I had a long talk with Jerry Garcia, and by long I mean a whole entire afternoon. We were stuck on this boat together, a Hell's Angels boat party up the Hudson River—'scuse me if you've heard this before. It was a long, hot day, and as we cruised the river the smog was so thick we could see either the Jersey side or the Manhattan side, but never both simultaneous. The air felt very thick and very deadly, and smelled like a dank bath towel with mold on it, left to rot behind the sink for a month. It seemed palpably clear that the planet— our common, y'know, *place*—was squeaking along more terminally by the month/week/hour/minute.

At one point we joked about the concept of "over the hill," wondering if once you're on the other side and rolling, picking up speed, whether it gets any easier (the "life" . . . the "living"): something to look forward to. (Jus' the sort of merry bulltickey people in their 20s and 30s are more or less *known for*.)

Over the hill: ha! It's not that it doesn't *work* that way— it's just too e-z a metaphor . . . too pat, too *bucolic*, too one-size-fits-not-much . . . a trio of words no more befitting our ultimate basic *predicament* than "good as gold" or "sure as moss grows on the north side of a tree."

Anyway, I *have* told the boatride story before, dozens of times probably . . . I repeat myself, OK? In this book alone, I talk about my pecker way too much . . . and the Beatles (gulp). I squawk about "high" and "low" it must be 13 times. I mention Kerouac a lot . . . Handsome Dick Manitoba . . . Ed Wood, of course.

I'm not gonna go for the "geezer disclaimer" (that I, uh, lose track of things), no no . . . I'm just not a perfectionist anymore, an artso nitpicker. Every single utterance can't be bran' new—what silly vanity. (If once I was Mozart, let me now be Haydn.) I'm too over & beyond *some* sort of divide to be concerned with such claptrap (it seems preposterous now that I ever was).

So you don't hold it against me, tho—and I in turn hold it against *you*—let's try and play it this way:

You can't fault me for having *pet themes and reference points*, can you? They crop up so often (in the v. same words, even) because, well, they're IN ME!—as John Lee would say—and they gotta come out. So why don't we simply think of this re-peat biz as my SET LIST? Like Jerry's 30-year bar band, the G. Dead, I *swear* I will never play the same exact set twice, OK? Hey, I won't abuse the prerogative!

OK?

OK?

Thank you.

But let me clear up a couple of bookthings.

The phantom album alluded to in "Dust" is unreleased no more. *St. Cecilia: The Elektra Recordings* by the Stalk-Forrest Group, as Blue Öyster Clot were known for 10 or 11 minutes, finally got CD'd, in a limited pressing, by Rhino/Handmade. It's actually pretty good, at least as good as the average

Quicksilver album—the BÖC's only documentation as a psy-chedelic combo. Hey—I wrote seven songs.

And then a big, big fuckup: NORMAN MAILER. In "The Wisdom in Our Underwear," I claim there's nothing by Norman in the *Rolling Stone Book of the Beats*, but that's only 'cause I didn't look close enough. He's got something on p. 281 (a paragraph on Allen Ginsberg). I'd say, "Fuck *me*"—it would only be proper—but I've used that expletive cluster too frequently already—so lemme just concede that I BLEW IT.

When I refer to "Reagan and Bush and Clinton" in "The Old Fuckeroo," that's Bush/Sr. I'm talking about (in case you're wondering).

Other than right here & now—this sentence—there is no explicit mention of 9/11/01 anywhere in the book, though its impact can doubtless be felt in some later sections of my title piece, which I finished in October '01. If the events of that day, along with the beginnings of their transformation of our national reality, had somehow occurred a couple years soon-er, it all would certainly have had a place in "Wisdom," my rambling take on the meltdown of the 20th century. Still and all, nothing that has gone down since would make me change a word of that ramble.

I have no interest in being all things to all people, any more than I do in being a rockandnothingbutwriter or the new Leopold Stokowski, and if you happen to be a supporter of the Patriot Act and/or the napalming of Iraqis or affiliated peoples, you should probably be reading someone else's book.

If, beyond that, you're flying the r*e*d w*h*i*t*e a*n*d b*l*u*e and aren't a veteran of Double-U Double-U Two, or if you voted for Bush/Jr. and intend to do so again, get your fucking nose OUTTA my book, like now, y'hear?

Hey: even if you're one of those folks who get their JOL-LIES being fooled all of the time, I ain't gonna be the one to try and fool you. Pull your own chain, chump! (I am not, in my next intro, gonna say I was joking.)

Oh, and I don't wear contact lenses anymore (by the way).

RICHARD MELTZER
Portland, 2003

GENERIC DEATH POEM

They live
they live
and they die

They live
they live
and they die

John Coltrane (Nancy Sinatra) (etc.)
lived and he's (she's) (they're)
dead (irreplaceable)
        (will be sorely missed)

                    etc.

AUTUMN RHYTHM

HAIKU #1

where the fuck's my car?
don't even gotta be drunk
no more t' lose it!

GIG

Let it be known, to begin with, that I didn't ask for this,
but was *asked*—

Assigned, in exchange for a sum equal to roughly a season's rent, the chore of composing a first-person account of
the process of aging (heh heh), "growing old" . . . of copping
in print to *being* old: an official GEEZER GIG.

My reluctance at first was natural. "I'm not there yet," I
protested. "But I'll start taking notes, OK?" (Had an editor or
two "noticed something" 'fore I did?)

Mainly, I felt, I've for damnsure got better things to do
than write about my current writhe-and-squirm; more viable

hoops to jump through than finding adequate voice to critique my ease or difficulty, for inst, in maintaining an unassisted daily bowel movement. At my age, who the hell's got *time* to waste on such twaddle?

Fuh . . .

Inevitabilities are a pisser to sidestep. Geezerhood comes when it comes—fuggit—but just as inev' as suddenly, finally being there, now!, on the cusp of fucking dotage, my time/left measured in thimbles not buckets, was that I would be invited—cajoled—roped into writing about it.

Writers are a vain buncha geeks, y'know? We don't always wear lampshades on our heads, but we do wear hats galore, funny and straight, to get our idiot-share of attention. A sucker for such bullcrap, I have worn one guise in particular, oh, a couple hundred times at least: The Naked Writeboy.

FULL-SERVICE nakedness! Wall-to-wall INTROSPECTION! A plethora of unembellished SELF: mind! heart! body! soul!—the whole burrito!

With so tacky a calling card, it was given that I would someday be recruited, for the usual mess of pottage, to stand naked in the freezing chill of geezer sempiternity, stripped of all warming, sheltering age-coded conceits: no more *pretending* to be old, or pretending to be young (for the sake of "narrative" fun & games!) . . . just being old and seeing old—with tired, squinty (as opposed to merely jaded) eyes.

What a dandy ultimate USE of the subject/object self: as a touchstone of Decline and Fall . . . mammal . . . human . . . universal! What sort of writer would I be to decline the invitation? Of all the cheesy stories I've wanted no part of, this would appear to have my name—well, one of 'em—all over it. The No-Insulation Kid at your service! *Deeper* than skin-naked, *deeper* than flesh-naked: come have a peek, see what's underneath . . . parts-o-me that age ain't touched, and those it's already trampled.

And hell yeah—independent of all this—I do have some copious THOUGHTS on the geezer "issue" . . . microminutiae to explore and explicate . . . lingering personal baggage, nasty and not, to get off my chest given so cheery a context.

Hey, I may not be *quite* there yet—a frigging "senior"—but time is definitely a-wasting, pottage needs to be procured, fiber to be ingested, and other stories to be writ . . . let's get on with it.

GEEZEROLOGY

Tomorrow used to be another day, or so somebody said. It ain't no more.

You're an old fucking foop, it's finally kicking in, and things can only get worse. Dry patches dot your face. Your eyebrows grow out weird: trim them *good*, bub, or look like some German Expressionist KOOK. There are hairs on your fucking *earlobes* back so far you can't see 'em, your eyes are so bad. Watch out—take care!—or you'll chip another tooth on a bowl o' banana flakes. T for Tuesday—don't forget—the day to take out the Trash. (Or izzit Thursday?) Oldfriends have had enough of YOU, and you've had enough of THEM, and on days like today you can't wait for them all to be bones in the boneyard. Be patient, it'll come, and in the meantime: clothing calls.

DAYS

The first Bukowski title I ever noticed in a bookstore was *The Days Run Away Like Wild Horses Over the Hills*. I was maybe 26, and it struck me as a tad corny. It wasn't that I didn't, um, appreciate the concept, the metaphor, this image of them galloping way off in a pack, leaving a mighty puff of dust, never to be seen again 'cept as dots on the horizon, or that I regarded it as hokily "romantic" or some such—our common mortality in prewar cowboy-flick drag—it just seemed (and in some ways still does) like hambone literary caprice: a self-designated "old man" coming on "old and wise." He was like 48 or 49 when it was published.

At 26, I didn't think much about eventually being 49. If I did at all, it was simply in arithmetic terms—that it would take me 23 years to get there. Who'd've thought it would only take 9 or 10? In life, ha, 'rithmetic works existentially. Over the hills! gone! . . . fuckadoodle.

Today, seven years beyond 49, it hits me like a two-by-four in the face. The days run, they don't walk, and not just the days, plural—the YEARS—but each and every 24-hour day. A couple years ago I started quantifying what a day actually felt like, what its duration as lived existentially *was*, and the unit day, I surmised, was only four hours long.

It now feels about three and a half.

The compression doesn't seem so much existential anymore as corporeal. Strictly physical factors have risen to the fore. For a while I've been aware of an upswing in basic bodily fatigue . . . lethargy . . . enervation. Lately, howev, it's also impacting my ability to handle the specifics of my so-called job, one more ostensibly mental than physical, to focus on th'm or pay even semi-continuous attention. The body part of mind has taken command and thrown in the towel.

Shoot—I'm a privileged fuck who stays at home and *writes*, and *I'm* feeling this beat. If I worked on an assembly line, being 56 would be devastating.

What can you get done in three and a half hours? (Better not piss too much—that'll cut it to three.)

LIFETIMES

One afternoon when I was 6 or 7, I sat around with some neighborhood kids watching a purple crayon with the paper removed float in a bowl of water. When it didn't dissolve immediately, nor after an hour or more, we figured it must be a matter of days, not hours—and only when days had *elapsed* would we know for sure.

After five days, having paid no notice for the previous four, I emptied what water was left and put the crayon, none the worse for wear, back in its box. In ensuing playtimes with these same kids I never bothered to bring it up. (I was the only scientist, mad or not, the only stickler for empirical doo-dah

in the bunch, and I knew even then that empiricists were
saps, killjoys and worse.)

A lot of things won't dissolve in *anything,* but it may take
a lifetime to know for sure . . .

Storage batteries.

Love and loss.

Friendship and betrayal.

Forty-year-old used condoms.

The complete works of Judith Krantz.

The concept of a perfect blowjob.

"I'm cuckoo for Cocoa Puffs" as pure prosody.

Richard Nixon's stench.

Or maybe, just maybe, they'll dissolve in EVERYTHING
. . . it jus' takes more than a single lifetime to see.

LIVES

All we get is dashed hopes, mangled and bungled dreams.
Is this good or bad?

TROPIC OF NIPPLES

Baby!—

*In my spare time, when not busy being old or jerking off or
worrying about my cat, I've been working on a nice little con-
traption to, uh, spank you with . . . and for you to spank me. It's
kind of a composite of things, and when I'm done it'll produce a*

nice little sting different from any of the whatsits we used last time.

Hey babe, I can't WAIT to sting your funky li'l geezer butt with it!

BEAT ME

Much as I like grocery lists, Jim Carroll beat me to "People Who Died," so I won't even list all my friends who are dead.

GEEZEROLOGY (2)

Every day, rain or shine, you see them, chugging down the avenoo—paunchy, stoopy, prune-faced, droopy, drooly—what a scene! Two and three abreast they come, clogging sidewalks with their arthrickety tortoise-dawdle: geezers on parade!

Indeed, there is much to be amused by in the street-face of geezerhood, but nothing more amusing than the shirts, skirts, pants, hats, jackets, socks, sneakers and umbrellas they mix and match with no regard for optical or even seasonal suitability—pinstripes w/ polka dots—team logos w/ tie-dyeds—purple w/ luminescent orange—Xmas plaids in June—what a scream!

Go 'head and laugh, they *are* a scream. Clowns and rock stars never dressed so funny. All your LIFE you've laughed at geezers and their clotting, make that clothing; made grievous light of their esthetic impairment; gotten your jollies at their feeble expense. Well, laugh while you can, buddy, but don't laugh *too* hard . . . 'cause someday soon the geezer will be YOU.

So listen up.

A recent survey by the Gerry Studies Department, Lewis and Bob College (Kliquot, New Hampshire), strips bare a prevalent MYTH concerning geezer clothes. The principal reason, previously overlooked, underestimated, or anyhoo underreported, for howcome they "dress so silly" is not so much their taste in attire is "alien or bizarre"—"f'r shit"—"up their ass"—as it is, simply, that these are the ONLY DUDS GEEZERS HAVE LEFT. Inotherwords, unless they are or were "total doofs to begin with," the report sez, chances're likely they once owned and wore not only sillystuff—hey, everybody needs *some* sillystuff—but one or more "neat" clothings (relatively speaking) which *because* they were neat got worn more frequent, thus wearing 'em OUT, leaving the geezer ultimately with his or her most *un*desirable garments, the threads they themselves cared for least—and now 'cuz of fixed income, alzheimer's, immobility or indifference, the hideous dregs is all they got left: their final apparel, their final "look." If they shop anymore it's at thrift stores, known repositories of the dregs of others live & dead, further prolonging the "cycle of dregdom." Hey, it makes sense.

Additional factors include: too FAT to wear yer own neatstuff no mo', dropping it from the active wardrobe, replaced by any uggle that still fits, or donning the former in uneasy "geezer defiance," running the risk—the study further claims—of "lookin' like an M-F'ing dipshit"; too skinny (same deal); bald or balding, in the case of formerly wearable hats and headgear, causing the 'gear to slipflop down, perching heavily on the ears, which flap out like turkey wings (hooty HAH!—'scuse my laffin' . . . it's just so *funny*); cataracts and blindness, requiring others to dress you, "often with sarcastic intent." It's not a pretty sight.

Jesus.

And what, for the merry love-o-Mike, might be DONE?

For geezers already there, very little. But for pre-geezers of virtually any stripe or stroke, a series of pre-emptive options, while hardly immense—and rarely pleasant—presents itself for P-G perusal.

GEARS, DUDE

What're those things they got in cars and watches, all sort-sa machinery, they have these little protruding, those y'know they're like spines coming off a circle, um, a wheel . . . a wheel with *levers*, that's what the, uh . . . HOW CAN I NOT KNOW WHAT THEY'RE CALLED?!?!

PRIORITIES

They've shortened the playing field, see. Less time also means less space. No more 80-yard passes, that's for sure, and no screen plays, no pulling guards, no double reverses . . . nothing calling for much in the way of finesse. No plays to waste, nor time to review strategy. What follows each snap of the ball is much the same—in derisive '40s parlance, "three yards and a cloud of dust."

Just punch it out, hit the line, *execute*—leather helmets, no face masks. Oomp. Oof. Blppp. Kuh-fmmp.

Thirty years ago, when the field was the size of Montana, and a lifetime seemed a reasonable span for pulling off something akin to literary fame & fortune, I fancied I would average a book and a half a year for all the years I saw spread before me—the approximate rate I was writing 'em at the time. If all had gone well, that would've meant 45 books over these three decades—hey, there are people who've done it!

As it stands today, I've had, I dunno, 10 or 11 books published, which still ain't too shabby. Since the last two are prob'ly the best I've ever done, it wouldn't *totally* shatter me if somehow they turned out to be the last two, period. But I imagine there *will* be more, although right now I'm not sure what shape, form or flavor any of them might conceivably take. If I live another 10–12–15 years, considering how tough it is for me to write these days, how long it takes, I'm looking at another three–four books, max. Or let's just even say three, or two . . . and I've GOTTA make those count—got to! got to!—not in terms of my "permanent record," my "legacy," but simply . . . between me and me. In some as yet unknowable way. Someday fairly soon I will have to decide: what the bleeping fuck will these books be?

Even less than 30, less than 25, the pipe dreams came fast and furious, and I actually believed, given proper exposure, that in due time I would cop a Nobel—well goodbye to all that. Goodbye to even that goodbye . . . what a load off my postadolescent mind.

I will certainly never be rich or anything close, but I wouldn't mind, just once, briefly, making what could pass for a middleclass income. (The guy who does my taxes has promised me the high-sign the moment I threaten to knock on that door.) But even that is more "symbolic" than anything anymore—and of what, I can barely remember—a silly oldschool notion I'm already half-set on letting go of f'rever.

Many waters under many bridges, and many letting-gos, great and small, present, past and future . . .

Is it necessary, for ex., even once by accident, that I ever be slim or trim again? That I regain the muscle tone I last had when I worked out regularly, oh, like 15–16 years ago?

Between now and the final curtain, does it mean a ding dang duck dick if I comb my hair? Shower and shave more than three times a week?

How strongly does self-esteem (or is it egotism?) compel me to continue wearing contact lenses, to bother correcting my eyesight to 20/20?

Does it matter that I rarely know who won a given year's Super Bowl? That I can no longer recite the line of succession to the heavyweight title? Would it matter if I *could*?

Does it mean shit to a shithook if I answer even one letter in 10, one e-mail in 50?

If I never again hear the Zombies' "Is This the Dream?"— does *that* matter?

Does *anything* absolutely, unequivocally matter?

Well yes, of course, LOVE matters, but how do you get it (how do you GET IT?) ('specially w/out grooming or shaving or muscles)—and how do you keep it f'r longer than it takes to brew a cup of tea? If I never get it, never find it again, I reckon I'll live . . . and if I die unloved, well, it's not like I've NEVER LOVED, y'know? My mem'ry is still pretty good in that regard—I could tell you old girlfriend tales till you puke. If I write another novel, maybe I'll tell 12 or 20.

PRESSURE DROP

A couple years ago, I had my hemorrhoids snipped, scraped, or whatever they do . . . something with a knife . . . the final surgical solution.

Though longer than I expected, as a hospital stay it wasn't so horrible. True, they botched their own estimate of when I'd be released, which threw a mean curve at my care & feeding. Instead of salad, fruit and, I dunno, oat bran or something, they fed me roast beef, potatoes and vanilla pudding, hotcakes and sausage—there'd been no plan drawn up for feeding me at all. Don't wanna lay on the hyperbole, but a day later, at home, it was like trying to shit a football . . . with severely challenged equipment . . . oh well.

But the stay itself, hey . . . I had this really pretty nurse who gave me demerol and changed my ass dressing. "This is gonna hurt," she warned, yanking the adhesive, "but nowhere as bad as *bikini waxing*"—she then apologized for being "superficial" . . . what a sweet, attractive person to have change your ass dressings.

Compared to what I'd envisioned, it was more like a weekend at a country club, a far cry from this scene in *Wild Angels* which had always plagued me, the one where Bruce Dern, strapped to a bed, lies dying with all these tubes in his arm. When I first saw it in the '60s, high on pot, I thought *Sheesh, I do NOT wanna die with fucking tubes in my arm.*

This wasn't anything like that, plus I learned that my blood pressure was high, but not *dangerously* high. I'd known for years it was high, and controlled it at times (in theory or practice) with exercise and diet. In any case, it was down from my previous reading, taken at an ER I dragged myself to when a spider bite got infected and blew up like a golf ball. (Maybe all the huffpuff I'd exerted helping a bookstore guy move all his stock, loading and toting too many things myself, is what lowered it.)

Hey, I don't even know what exactly you GET from high blood pressure—heart attack? stroke? I don't know—honest!—and obviously I should; is it denial or stupidity (stubbornness?) not to know such shit at 56? But it was down, so *good*.

Or *is* it good?

Strokes I don't want—who does? But are heart attacks all bad? They come in handy sometimes—a quick end, unlike AIDS or cancer—but if they don't kill ya outright, a freaking hospital is still your destiny. Open heart butchery . . . quintuple bypass . . . sheesh-a-mighty.

Whatever.

But really, strapped down or not, I DON'T wanna die in a freaking hospital . . . hideous surroundings & lighting . . . mean or kind or indifferent personnel, with or without the bikini waxing . . . all variety of tubing in my arms. I don't!

Once you're dead you're dead, but still: why relinquish the calling of shots before that? So I should prob'ly do some homework.

HAIKU #2

periph'ral vision?
bicycles slower than me
run over my feet

THE SHIT TOGETHER

I forget the title or the publisher (HarperCollins? Random House?), but a few months ago some 25-year-old kid—'scuse me—grownup asked me to contribute to a book he'd somehow scammed a contract for. Something on the order of "advice to the next generation." He invited me 'cause I seemed, in some conspicuous way, a representative of the previous (or pre-previous) (certainly not current) generation. Here's what I gave him:

Well, OK, let's get clear on one thing: there are no "generations." Maybe once, but no longer. Or, if you'd like, there is only one. We're all in the shit together. Period.

To cut to the chase, American Youth has never had fewer advantages—assets—resources. Not in all the time I've been around, and that includes the loathsome, despicable *pre*-rock fifties (when they banned comic books, and the *best* you could look forward to was wearing a tie every day of your life). Aside from the extra years you've got remaining, your lot is basic NOTHING. Youth is a dismal sick joke today: a consumer-demographic blip *defined* as maimed and retarded.

Quickly, you're gonna need to think for yourself (or perish!), come up with your own system (no cheating!): it's fucking compulsory.

And then, the long run. Though miracles do happen, it will in all likelihood take you longer than you anticipate—an unfair percentage of the time you've got left—to get much of anything right, to develop your own "chops," to arm yourself the way nurturing parents *hypothetically* did while you were (or at least *I* was) still wriggling in diapers . . . you have to factor in the LONG HAUL. (Writing, for inst—something I personally wouldn't wish on a dog—will take you *fifteen years*, minimum, to even begin to get right.)

In the meantime, an early order of biz: unplug from the cyber lifeline . . . it's a fucking *deathline*: the bitter END of mammal life as any of us have ever known it. And encourage—by hook, crook, or outright subterfuge—everybody ELSE to unplug, y'hear?

And the next order, well, choice of poison. There's no getting very deep into this thing-called-life without the faithful assistance of whatsems that at least *partially* will also be killing you. For symptomatic relief, artificial energy, access to alternate universes, superficial kicks, whatever . . . there's no getting around 'em. Still, it would be hokey to impose my actual tastes on you, like you should drink, say, a lot of strong bitter ale with lots of hops—avoid red wine until a doctor orders it—whiskey will slow you down, put you to sleep—if you're of a mind to do tobacco, better to chew it . . . no, I won't do that. But if you're young enough, speed probably isn't such a bad idea. Heroin and the opiates, on the other hand, really aren't for kicks—they're for *heavy* grief reduction.

Speaking of which, from experience, I would say there's really only one viable program of low-to-mid grief reduction (don't laugh): the blues. Equip yourself—listen to everybody from Charlie Patton to Son House to Memphis Minnie to Robert Wilkins to Robert Johnson to Elmore James and Muddy Waters, Lightnin' Hopkins, John Lee Hooker (pre–1960), Howlin' Wolf, Little Walter . . . all the way up to like Otis Rush, Albert Collins and, okay, Jimi Hendrix. (No Robert Cray.) (And no Stevie Ray Vaughan.) At its best, and I'm not talkin' semi-best, rock as a means to that desired end is a semi-reprise of the blues (never the full dose).

Buddhism? I wouldn't know, some Beats swore by it, but I've never tried it.

Speaking of Beatniks, don't read *On the Road*, not ahead of four or five other Kerouac titles: *Big Sur*, *The Subterraneans*, *Tristessa*, *The Dharma Bums*, and this one you never heard of called *Vanity of Duluoz*.

Otherwise, I dunno, see the movie *Mesa of Lost Women*—don't ask me why. (I'm sure it's rentable.)

That's it, so anyway, once again: 'tain't no generations. Any more than there are "decades." But some *very* deep shit. "If it ain't shit, it ain't IT"—somebody French said that. Get used to it.

ANYTHING

How many people die having embraced and experienced one thing on their own terms for ten minutes? How many die having popped a pimple perfectly . . . once?

NEVER

A position you'll never shake me from:

Even in better possible worlds than this one, to inflict the full slimy wrath of your being (and its ongoing shadow and stand-in, your neurosis) on a living creature more vulnerable than yourself is despicable. Or let's just say unwise.

As far as I know, I've had no children. The buck stopped with me.

VANITY AND CULTURE

Am I really and truly, by a stretch of anyone's imagining besides my own, a beatnik drunk, as I'm fond sometimes of I.D.'ing myself?

A philosopher on a barstool?

A philosopher at all?

A real drunk, even?

My buddy Nick always said if you can't drink through a hangover, you're no drunk nohow. Well I can't make it through 'em—they drop me in my tracks. Nor do I share with Bukowksi fans a fondness for the designation "old drunk" (ho hum) . . . what a quaint cartoon. But I do get a good portion of my kicks these days in bars, where two-three afternoons a week I'll sit and swill down pints as bitter as life itself—and if that sounds corny, well, tough. (Hey, people!—JOY is involved.)

I'd rather have a meaningful conversation with a stranger or friend in a dark, gloomy dive than most anything in this here life, and I'd certainly rather run an idea 'round a barroom than beat it to death on paper . . . turn it into a fucking essay.

I don't "get ideas" from drinking, and anything I write down drunk I usually can't even read later. Ideas as experienced, as groped and sussed out *in vivo*—in life—are of far greater oompah to me than ideas "themselves," and it ain't just the dialogue—the back & forth, the alcohol-accelerated fervor—that makes suss-out in bars so appealing, it's the alc-assisted finitude and *termination*.

No, I'm not talking finite in the extended sense, y'know, like mortality, death—the end of it ALL—but finite in the here & now, as a limit-line and cutoff to further (let's call it) intellection, intelligizing. Alcohol in real time can be my-t all reet for serving you the warrant *This far is far enough*. Twenty years ago, when I still occasionally wrote drunk, what it basically meant was an end to endless revision, especially simpy things like word choice. *Pick a word, damn it, and we're done!* (More "definitive" than this—why bother?)

The provisionally so, the functionally so, is all you need in the way of an afternoon's so-ness . . . no carry-over to next week (and *phuck* eternity). Another of alc's great gifts: the GRACE to embrace a bottom line of so-ness.

And this is even *without* delivering euphoria, or nirvana, or oblivion—it ain't heroin!—without actually blunting the ideational *edge*: an edge you're gonna need, right?, 'cause you WANT it to keep a-knockin' at your being, to "trouble" you enough to command your ongoing, if slip-sliding, attention. Hopefully, ideally, what you get in the process is a glimmer, as well, of an idos's own attrition. Discourse and disintegration in a single dose. (Did I say I wasn't pushing one poison over all others? Pardon me.)

There was a run of maybe 20 years where I drank for very ferocious reasons, then another five where I stayed at home, wrote, and drank hardly at all, but today it's one of the calmest things I do. Where once I behaved antisocially when even halfway drunk, I now behave *socially*. Sociably. (You could ask anyone.) Which could mean *I've* gotten calmer . . . or maybe just sleepier.

Rarely do I drink at home, and the only homestuff that might be lacking in bars is my own music. My goddam collection. You're not gonna hear *New York Eye and Ear Control*, or even "Ornithology," at the Snake & Weasel. But if there's any kind of jukebox, the difference between a very specific this and a that isn't gonna be the make-or-break of a couple-three hours on a stool. No Doors, no Stones before *Black and Blue*, but lookit—George Jones! . . . let's hear "Open Pit Mine."

And if there isn't a juke, and all you can reasonably expect from one of those crummy, nuthin' compilation-X tapes some barperson made is one tune in ten that even semi-works as soundtrack for the drunken moment, as expedient grist for a nuance of conversation or the random tweaking of your pliant mindset, that's a-plenty. Music in a bar is music *in context*, and one in ten is okey doke.

In general, the whole basic shuck of cultural "choice" has lots more resonance, both volitionally and phenomenological-ly, in beer joint Z than a supermarket or record store, a mul-tiplex movie house. Even if the options are this pisswater brew versus that (Bud and Hamm's, let's say, with no IPA in sight), or the yes/no/yes/no of *maybe* coming on to a new face down the bar you've got no chance in hell of doing the meat-dance with, not if you were the last bozo on earth . . . ha . . . at least you're eyeball to eyeball with the NOTION of getoff, in ballpark range of its being not some distant illusion (a cockamamie *abstraction*), but oboy, all the diff. in the world: a CURRENT ILLUSION.

To grab some jargon from the existentialists, with a cou-ple-three Hamm's in your gut—hell: even Coors fucking Lights—potentiality begins to *approximate* actuality, starts behaving (in raw, wretched ways) quitelike it. 'Tain't even *vir-tual* getoff—rocks-off, a "real" beer buzz—of course, but something ASYMPTOTIC to it: curves stretching to languid infinity, or midway through a raingrey afternoon, can bring you *close enough*.

Attraction/repulsion, acceptance/rejection: with even 3rd-string ethyl enhancement factored in, such pairings no longer seem so either/or, so monochromatically binary . . . just a standard ration of flavors and colors from the same wheezy "interactive" gestalt.

Two bar-trains running. So some funkysweet babe says nuh nuh NO to your overture of whoopee, okay? Well, phoo, fie, fug a donut, but HEY!, without missing a beat, without really changing the subject (one "text" equals another), you can likewise reject Beethoven's 9th, "Be-Bop-a-Lula," all the works of D.H. Lawrence—while you're at it, THE ENTIRE WESTERN CANON—or, conversely, you can accept NOTH-ING, literally.

Nothing! If there's enough sweat to the experience, total wipe-out is as good as a score . . . it *is* a score. From *gimme! gimme!* to *nada? I like it!* . . . a most plausible leap . . . or maybe that's just me in my sleepiness. Or my geezer serenity. Or whatever.

I may fancy myself a thinker, but I never said I was smart. I was in my 50s before I realized barmaids flirt with you not 'cause they think you're cute or respect your wisdom, but to get a bigger tip. But I *always* overtip—usually a buck a beer, regardless of the act they do or don't throw my way—though it's possible I don't jack off thinking about them as much as I did before learning their cruel secret.

The culture of no-choice: the fetor of a men's room urinal is the highest—and lowest—and most median in culture-hands as dealt . . . the universal haps. Any bar, meantime, where the TV is never off should be NAPALMED.

GEEZER DATE

Oh FUDGE—midnite and I'm outta Viagra! Wait . . . Walgreen's might be open.

Be right back—don't go 'way!—and long as I'm there, might as well get some fresh Depends, I'm durn near outta them too, and what's that one you, uh . . . Prevail?

Ooh babe, it tingles my SHORTHAIRS to think it: you 'n' me mixin' the mature (the ripe!) and the infantile . . . the autumn (the winter!) and the not-even-spring! So effing WHAT if we can't control our functions? Weewee . . . doodoo . . . you can change me and I'll change you!

Oh darlin', let's really make a mess!

FROM R.D. TO U.S.G.

Ten years ago, I looked like Robert De Niro, the *young* Robert De Niro. I now look like Ulysses S. Grant.

MODELS (1)

My cat. Who is dying. Or not. Can't be sure.

For the time being, living.

He's 17 and his kidneys are shot and his thyroid is fucked and he's got the beginnings (at least) of arthritis. The weather stinks and the food stinks and he complains all the time.

He doesn't *know* he's dying, dig it, any more than he knows he's "old"—a notion both too abstract *and* concrete to be of any use to him. He does, however, seem all too aware that he's LOSING IT. A window sill only two feet off the floor is now a difficult jump for him. He hasn't got the spring he once did, and unless his timing is perfect he'll blow it. This *maddens* him—he meows loudly . . . howls! . . . flashes me his what-the-*hell*-is-going-on? look. I rap on the sill to encourage another try, but he rarely goes for it. Too proud to suffer assistance, he'll promptly jump down if I lift him up there. Never chases moths or flies anymore—can't keep up with 'em.

Lately he's cleaning himself less . . . could there be too little saliva to spare? When it gets really hot he does no grooming at all, and by the time he gets to it, with all the accumulated sweat, his coat is stiff and matted. He picks at it with his teeth and gets nowhere, mopes and moans and sits around looking, oh—what's that stupid, cutesy cat-word?—scruffy.

Has his weight gone down because his appetite is failing, or might Fancy Feast, which was shit to begin with, be getting worse? Every time I open a can, a given flavor, it looks different, smells different, from a few weeks before—am I imagining things? When he walks away from Savory Salmon Feast, a former favorite, I defer to *his* taste and open something else, but in what LANGUAGE can I deal with his blaring bewilderment, his sense of world-gone-fucking-wrong? It maddens *me* that I can't 'splain to him the snuffout of quality control (they get their salmon in the sewer, see), the unregulated exploitation of poor contingent beings (they don't care if you live or die).

The depth of my feelings for the little beast tears me apart. My sidekick, my pal, the first and only pet I've had with hair (if pet is really the word—I've always thought of him as heck, an equal), he's also the last. I won't be doing this number again. Why oh why, I ask, did I allow myself to get so viscerally involved with a warm-blooded earthling who neither speaks nor understands a known human tongue, who can't be asked "Where does it hurt?" or even "How many fingers?," and certainly hasn't the means of volunteering such biz on his own? It tears my guts out that I can't tell him anything he'll understand 'bout how come he can't go outside no more.

The most colossal of his losses—by his reckoning, surely—and he didn't lose it, I took it. A tough guy, a fighter, he was getting in too many fights, which led to too many abscesses, which more than anything is what killed his kidneys. A bully when you get down to it, he could no longer take the meas-ure of every new stray on the block, every dog smaller than a doberman, and once or twice he came home *mangled*. For more than a year now, he's been confined to quarters, where I've been not only his keeper, his jailer, but worse than that: his torturer.

So much for equality.

Once a day, to flush out his toxins, I give him a dose of greenish fluid from an IV bag, 150cc dripped or squeezed through the hole I poke with an inch-long needle in the loose skin of his back. Every time I poke him, he *yelps* . . . betrayal, anyone? Some claim that cats/dogs "know" when you're help-ing them . . . dunno. While the months go by and he's still liv-ing and—who can tell?—maybe in gen'ral hurting less, he's yet to stop yelping, and after I release him he lunges from my lap and scampers to the door, where he sniffs at the crack and cries.

OUT THERE: where all the goodtimes were. Wild youth, wild maturity. Anything-but-mellow middle age. The long hot run of a life/lived. Where he lived it all 'cept for inconse-quentials like meals in cat-bowls and sleep. This geezer had his run.

Besides all the fights, and he really *was* pretty good vs. dogs (claws to the snout!—first strike preferred), he did his share of mouse catching, bird catching, tree and phone-pole climbing, blind leaps down open manholes, dashes up/down schoolyard fences in thunderstorms, and I saw him one time scale a 30-foot ladder, the kind with narrow rungs, to a roof where hot tar was being laid down, emerging (much later) and descending unscathed. Fond of vehicles, he enjoyed splitting up a single urination and directing its stream at the hubcaps of three separate cars, though hardly ever the *first* three—he was selective—and crawling in windows of tall trucks to smell the upholstery and piss on the steering wheel.

And, shoot, he must've gotten *some* kicks (or he wouldn'ta done it) from his afternoons just hangin' out with me—interspecies "male bonding," alright?—the zillion times I brought a chair outside and sat with him as I doodled over the morning's writing. I'd sit and he'd sit, an hour, two hours, after which I'd follow him on his prowl, see him terrorize the neighborhood.

Now it's like he's in a nursing home.

Perched up there in his window seat, he gets very agitated when he spots a sparrow on a branch or a cat, 'specially one he used to beat on, roaming free. Whenever visitors come by, he follows the scent of street grit tracked in on their shoes, nuzzles mini-blades of grass fortuitously caught in a rut in the floor. On bright afternoons, he finds a suitable patch of light on the rug and settles there—as if he were outside. His fur is dark and the sun fries him like a biker in black leathers, dehydrating him worse than he already is, undercutting the day's forcefeed of liquids. I could close the blinds, natch, but what sort of asshole would take such a treat away from him? ('Twould be like taking an 80-year-old smoker's pack-o-cigs.) I *won't* fuck with his dignity, not anymore, but for a while, if he also happened to be napping, I would sometimes move an object—a box, a large pillow—between him and the sun. When he woke to see this, he got extremely vocal, yowling in sheer exasperation.

But those yowls wurn't nothin' compared to the ones he did—and does—when the sun is down. A creature more of Night than of Day—for 16 years, it was when he was most independent, autonomous, most unimpededly *animal*—he's likeliest then to get mega-crazed about the fact of his imprisonment. Somewhere 'round midnight, the yowls become lonely wails—the volume goes up a notch, and the degree of urgency, until suddenly they're these ghastly, blood-curdling DISTRESS SIGNALS.

Which wake me, twitching, like no earthquake, no smoke alarm, no human caterwaul down the street, ever has, and I'm forced to wonder: Is he *dying*? Has a dire wolf broken in? Realizing that neither is the case, I figure maybe the s.o.b. has got his appetite back, he needs a fresh can of slop, or I forgot to clean the litter box, but it never seems to be anything that mundane, or that specifiably doable, but something more on the level of *Wake up, dammit! and hang w/ me in another room!* Or, I dunno, *Be around for me—c'mon!—you're the only friend I've got.*

Whether I comply or not (and usually I do), there isn't a night I don't lose sleep . . . as if I ain't tired enough.

Theoretically—if he can take naps, I can take naps—I could occasionally, prob'ly, make it up. More unsettling is his waking me out of dreams and I lose 'em. THE THIEF OF DREAMS!—add that to the list of things he'll never know about himself.

The little guy persists.

A fighter indeed, he's lasted six months longer than the vet's most optimistic forecast. He goes up and down, up and down, but he hasn't begun to give up the fight. One moment he's lying there grim and wasted, and I see the labored crawl of all livingthings to the Abyss. I leave the room, return, and he's walking on the keyboard of my computer—having hopped on a pile of books, from the books to a chair, then a table, and finally my desk—writing:

rdertffffffffff[]'
Erddddddd96+88opppppppppppppppp pjwawsa/8********
,mk'/Ohyguj][['=e\
erd--=dxi89uuuu 90oooooooolokkkkkl;.po;0000;'p89dfv
-0------gf7yht6\\\\tygr
yuhdfvfdrctrfrftddddddddddddddplooo

I hope, when I'm his age, I write as well.

DEVO PLAYS MENSA

Some people I know, more well-intentioned than not, keep offering to help set up a website for show-&-telling shards of my writing to a "wider audience," instantly rendering me "less invisible" (as if somehow I've been hiding), but I always decline. The prospect totally, utterly revolts me, but who knows?—maybe my arm will be twisted (peer pressure is like that), and sooner or later I'll relent.

If so coerced, and someday, sure enough, I find myself stuck with a frigging home page, the message right up front, way at the top, will be: *I've already lived life for real. How's about if I live it for fake?*

As imitations-of-life go, have any, writ large, been shabbier than the Internet? Shabby but clean, like all these dot-com nerds, the yuppie cocksuckers who caretake the action, pay far more heed to cleanliness than content; as shabby as death and not even real death, just death by default, by virtue of not-being-life . . . a room of dead mannequins . . . or daytime TV.

At its utter bottom-line "best"—most arch—at sites overseen by some o' your more *acid-headed* yuppie idiots—it has the look and feel of Devo at a Mensa convention . . . how groovy. At its worst—or in general—the trickle-down "populist" version—it's the acrylic sock section at Kmart.

What a giggle pit! . . . what a seedy "public world" to have served on a plate.

Listen, folks . . . I have online access 'cause as a writer it's now *mandatory*. Editors want instant delivery of the fruits of your labor. I never graze the Internet for anything like fun & frolic. But so you don't think I'm totally out of it, The Man From Yesterday, no fun nohow, there's a cyberpit I do drop in on from time to time: the English-language site of the Nihon Sumo Kyokai, the governing body of sumo—the only sport I follow anymore.

Http://www.sumo.or.jp/index_e.html . . . check it out . . .
six tournaments a year (the odd-numbered months)
. . . y'might find it a hoot.

NOTHING

There is nothing that concerns me less than the decor of
my own home.

D.C.

Diminished capacity.

Does 7 plus 4 equal 11, or does it equal 3?

Impaired mental acuity and memory miseries (short term
and long) and all that crap.

Who was the "New Journalist" who wrote the *Esquire* article on Joe DiMaggio . . . not Gore Vidal . . . not Vidal Sassoon
. . . what the hell was his name? Christ, it was *famous* . . . got
reprinted . . . fuggit.

And who's that German vibes player, uhh, played some
very out shit, had an album on ESP, lived in Woodstock
awhile? One-syllable last name . . . or is it two? Definitely not
Borah Bergman.

Or like I'll somehow remember the *complete* details of a
story I heard the other day—or earlier the same day—but
have trouble 'membering WHO told it t' me . . . can't put a
face (or voice!) on it.

When I saw Matt Dillon in *Drugstore Cowboy* whine about how hopeless it can get sometimes just having to tie your shoes, I thought: whudda stretch! 'Taint under *any* circumstances that difficult. Well . . . hoo! . . . as somethin' to even just *keep track of*, 'tis! I can go a quarter-mile without NOTICING mine're untied.

I'll be dog*gone* if the GEEZER EPISODES hain't been piling up. I'll go for a pizza and totally forget where I parked the car . . . *no idea*. Circle the block, all four streets, both sides, nope, so I walk the next block, and the next: where izzzzit?! Then a few days later the goddam battery dies 'cause I turned the headlights on, not off—in mid-afternoon. It'd been dark and rainy, see, but that was the *previous* aft. Hey— I knew I was s'posed to do *something* on-off-wise (I jus' got it wrong).

Then there's this nail that I missed, I was clipping 'em. Fourth finger, right hand, is that the ring finger? You go nail by nail by nail, left to right, how do you MISS ONE? I don't believe I ever missed one before . . . but whuddo *I* know?

It drives me infuckingsane.

And I can't balance my checkbook anymore to save my life, even with a calculator. Used to be a snap. And I can't pay bills on time, can't keep on top of the *chore* of paying them. I put 'em in a stack and the stack keeps stacking. Gets so daunting it's scary. How long before they shut off my power—or my sorry ass gets evicted?

Some holistic guy I ran into in a bar thought there might be a left brain/right brain aspect to it, y'know writing and then writing *checks*, going from the "creative" to the "practical," and he recommended I try the Hawaiian Haaaaaa Breath. Breathe in through your nose, deep, exhale through your mouth . . . *haaaaaaaa* . . . then in through your nose again: do the whole thing five times. Or was it ten? Well I've done it five, I've done it ten . . . ha ha haaaa. (Could it be he was putting me on?)

On somebody else's suggestion, I've started taking ginkgo, which I find makes me about five percent more alert, more able to cop to operational details—hey, I'll take it. ('S better than three percent.) She also mentioned bee pollen, but I can't recall if that had to do with alertness or the immune system. I shoulda wrote it down.

What I've gotta really do now is write EVERYTHING down, and leave all kindsa notes to myself ("gas for car" . . . "rent due Monday") where I'll be certain to see 'em, like on a chair I'm gonna use or the counter next to the fridge or on the bathroom floor . . . write 'em as soon as I *think* to write 'em— no waiting a sec!—or it'll be "Duh . . . whut wuz it I was *about* to write down???"

And as far as the alleged creative rubbish goes, I'm not so adept now'days at navigating even *one* side of my brain. G-g-gone is my ability to write on lotsa subjects simultaneous, bing bang bing—and it once was one of my stronger credentials. Working whole-hog at only TWO PIECES, two separate assignments, at the same time: no can do! Shifting gears from one to the other, I lose the thread of both, shoot my wad just finding my way back to either one of 'em, and after five paragraphs I feel like scrawling "To be continued." And continuing . . . . *later.*

I call on more subsets of myself to write than in days of old 'cuz I NEED to mobilize more parts of myself. If the mind can't do it alone, the heart hasta pull some nasty weight. We'll find out soon what capacity my heart has for write-muscle shitwork. Gonad writing? Well, there's that too, eh? (Whatever it takes.)

Jeez—it's gotten to where I can barely hack *worrying* about more than a couple things at once. A return-o-call I do *not* wanna make to an ex-girlfriend who wants a bigggg, agonizing favor of me; date with the dentist after not having gone for seven years: to add a third vexation and a FOURTH would produce neuro-overload. My system short-circuits, there's a maximum stress point.

And actual *crises* . . . whew! If I lost my keys and my glasses, that'd be one godawful bummer. If on top of that I lost my wallet—or my left shoe—or my fucksucking computer broke—it would effectively DEMOLISH ME. There's no way I could live another 15 minutes.

SAVAGE MEAT, PUNGENT MEAT
(UNDIMINISHED LUST)

you
want
show &
tell,
well:

the smell of a woman (any
woman) merely SUGGESTED BY
the smell (stink?) of me is
often sufficient to make me
abandon EVERYTHING

COOTIES

Ageism? *Heck* yeah, it exists. Is real. Rampant, even.

In the town where I live, *overt* racism, sexism and even classism, homophobia, anti-other-people's-cultural-et-cetera are fairly rare, which is to say that while many may harbor topical prejudices, manymost have at least become hep to the protocols of concealing and containing their public *expression* . . . but this does NOT seem so cozily the case with anti-geezer predilection. Lotsa folks, i.e., non-geezer folks, have developed no habits for biting their tongues in real-time verbal dealings with geezers, or even pre-geezers. When it comes to expressing, oh, certain particular point-blank *things*, geezers are still fair prey . . . they're open-season slow-moving targets.

As a pre-geezer, or a late pre-geezer, or an early geezer—whatever I am—I've been getting a taste of what's in store: a round of previews.

This guitarist I run into who always shamelessly sucks up to me, hoping maybe I'll write about him, egged me recently into telling a bunch of dumb stories 'bout my encounters with bands from before he was born, bands that later—

through recordings—he got to appreciate (and steal licks from). I was feeling generous, and he kept begging for more! more! more!, when suddenly he lost interest and snapped at me, all but kicking me in the nuts: "Enough of the old WAR STORIES already"—say what? . . . like I was some grim-sweaty Jack Lemmon or Jimmy Stewart getting weepy-eyed about D-Day. Then, to hype me on a new band he was getting together, he sez to me, with no irony whatsoev: "In your time, you'd have really liked us"—in my *time*?! Which you think is now all *up*? Well fuck YOU, shithead! (You also owe me 4 bucks.)

When I was 53, a 21-year-old stripper I'd been bouncing around with, and by bounce I'm talkin' mainly bar-hopping— I'd buy the beers, and sometimes she'd buy 'em—she told me at some point it wasn't "such a good idea" to chum around with somebody twice her age. "Shit," I said, cutting to the chase, "why don't you do the long division? I'm two and a *half* times your age—old enough, prob'ly, to be your grandpa." "Well, right . . . that's what I was saying." And therefore *what*—you don't cotton to the prospect of me DYING on you? Rather not be SEEN with a soon-to-be pruneface? Y'think I'm a fucking VAMPIRE sucking yer youth? (Well, honey, I'm not that nuts about yer youth.)

Hey!—whoa!—I could understand if I were some kind of boring old *nuisance* or something, a fool spouting antique vernac like "balderdash" or "jiminy christmas," but these jerks *wanted* a whiff of my seasoned p.o.v., fallout from my vast (um) experience, and they got off galore on my knowing-more-than-them—more than I got off on any of *their* finer qualities—& then in the end it's like I was just a prop, a curiosity, an "other" in their midst . . . they would rather be with their OWN KIND. Well, fine.

'S not like I take such treatment personally—I'd rather not consort with geezers either—but I do still have a degree of vitality left, I've got fun fun FUN up the old wazoo, so it doesn't really make too much sense to me. By no means am I covered with even a *thin* layer of dust yet, and to cut to the only chase that matters: so the hell WHAT if I *were* (and what happens when finally I *am*?)?

Really, boys and girls, I *don't* wanna be in a room full of geezers, but to no greater extent than I'd avoid one containing a gang of lawyers, or PGA golfers, or high school gym teachers, or evangelical missionaries, or Hollywood coke addicts, or podiatrists, or cops. Truly, I do *not* wanna be stuffed in dense with old coots and old farts—but I could certainly take 'em one or two at a time.

And like what's the score, anyway (irrational? rational?), on geezer anathema? How'd they get to be shunned like LEPERS, like homeless wretches outside yuppie espresso joints? What is it that compassionless cretins half their age (you know who you are!) have against them, f'r crying out loud?

Granted, in their endgame they don't move so fast, and to scuzzy judgmental types they might not look so fab, and they're fuck-hard at times to understand, and what about those eeky aftershaves they use? . . . but that don't begin to explain it.

Geezers are *needy*? Helpless, even? Well, much of humankind is helpless and needy . . . you ever see the band

Cat Power, Chan Marshall? They're sour, caustic, and bitter? You shoulda met the late-great M.T. Kinney at 25.

Is it simply, or chiefly, the STAMP OF ENDGAME emblazoned on the surface of their being? Itchy-twitchy evidence to young louts of their own mortality, of the literal way of all flesh and all flash? A case of shoot-the-messenger? Or would that be a mite too metaphoric—and teleological—and mightn't there be a little too much *denial* on young'uns' parts for such a leap-o-logic?

Or, after all is said and done, might it boil down to no more, no less, than the creeping ineffable: COOTIES?

Geezer cooties! (The way of all all.)

MY OWN SKIN

Though it appears feasible, seldom have I been able to write my way out of it. Oh! would it suit me to scram the "me" scene! More than likely, you need to be dead to pull it off.

ON-OFF

We would all, of course, be better off dead. Is that a truism or what?

No more pain, no more disappointment or responsibility, no more shit to fear, nothin'. The ultimate in relief and deliverance, the ultimate in slack-off. No more tumbling to the age-old con of "striving," no more lock-step or gimp-step to the fetish of "playing out your string."

Could death take your breath away with greater vicious-ness or greater *efficiency* than life itself already does?

If there's a problem anywhere, obviously it's not in the *being* dead—that part's e-z—but in the dying: the torment of having your action stamped CANCELED! . . . the cheap, vile drama of a useless bod tossing in the SPONGE . . . the per-petual fret over WHEN?, over HOW? . . . the white-knuckle wait 'til whate'er-the-bleak-fuck rounds the bend belching STEAM as it choo-choos straight at YOU to bulldoze you screaming in ag' every INCH of your last sleazy mile.

No: death ain't no-way the "great mystery" that dying is, and with suicide as an option, a tool—the anodyne in your pocket!—y'even get to specify the when and the how.

Don't know 'bout you, but I've thought of killing myself a good quarter to a third of the mornings of my life, faced with yet another day of IT, and my fair share of noons and nights as well, in direct response to unbearable obstacles (to sundry whatev) falling, lurching, wobbling in the way, for instance DEMONS. There's no living through them (it's inconceiv-able!), so why not blow everything that's blowable away? If you can't put out the fire, eliminate the matter. (They dyna-mite oil wells, don't they?)

Methods I've considered: bullet to the head, right side (I'm a righty); bullet through the eye (no preference left or right); jump from a tall building (the kind Superman used to leap in a single bound); normal hanging w/ rope; hanging w/ barbed wire 'round my neck. I've never entertained thoughts of *cut-*

ting my throat—it has a nice ring to it, though—nor of slicing my guts. These would require some finesse, and if you muff it, where are you?

Poison, f'rinstance cyanide? That can't be too pleasant. But pills, y'know, like valium or seconal—yeah, why not?

I've also fantasized a good shortlist of *un*doable scenarios—things you couldn't verywell do yourself—like an arrow in the face from 50 paces. (Wouldn't it be great to be *both* archer and target?) A railroad spike through the heart'd probably take more than one whack—plus you wouldn't exactly have the right angle—but that's definitely one I could feature. And it sure would be neat to throw your own severed head under the wheels of an oncoming truck . . . alone, you'd have to make it an unsevered one.

HERE's a nifty, baroque end-dream: to be poked through the heart by a spear weighted down by a TWO-STORY HOUSE. The inhabitants wouldn't have to leave. With so much weight, it would slide through you like a tusk through butter.

All that said, I must confess I meditate on suicide less than I used to—way less. Could it be that the concept has less reverb, less bombast, when you're actually near (or nearer) the end? You'd be surprised, but when it comes to putting the big gilt-edged *frame* around all this shit, life is quite a bit like wrestling—bombast plays a huge fricking part. Bombast and Romance.

Y'know, I'm as romantic as the next a-hole, but capital-R Romance as a NOTION, as an all-accommodating vehemence, has its time and its place, its stage and wardrobe, its

dance and its tune—and the bub-strut of *this* Romantic number is the proper toss-off of, oh—you guessed it—Callow
Youth.

Unless there's an immediate something to urgently deal
with—an inoperable nose tumor, let's say—suicide, like Trix,
is indeed for kids. As a fast-food solution, an objective to
aspire to, it's for people still in chapter 1 or 2 (no later than
3): grandiloquents young and vain enough to imagine they've
got SO! MUCH! MORE! to erase. (Been there, ahem, so I
know.)

In the later chapters, life on its own does a bloody fine job
erasing every massive slab of the dang shebang that genuinely counts. All that's left to efface is the declarative sentence "I
am living."

DON'T REMEM

Can anybody out there *please* help me?

Who (or what) is (or ever was) DOGGY JULIAN—or
possibly Doggie Julian?

Early to late 1960s.

(Possibly in a dream.)

HALF REMEM

"I am a soldier, big and strong. To some good boy I'll soon
be-long."

Or it might've been "sailor."

The earliest clump of text I even half remember . . . jeezus.

No, it's not some army/navy pedophile thing—or is it?—but a line from a Christmas play in the first or second grade. I was playing a *toy*, see. That would be 1951 or '52. The Korean War was on.

Wait, let me . . . uh . . . *first* grade.

Did I wear a soldier or a sailor suit?

Uhhhhhhhh.

Could it have been white? Blue? Khaki doesn't ring a bell.

GEEZEROLOGY (3)

So where were we? Ah, *yes*.

When we suspended our seminar on "geezer clothes," we were pondering the issue of solutions—stopgap or otherwise—sensible paths for pre-geezers imminently faced with the Wearing Of The Ug. In a nutshell, what it oozes down to is not one but TWO hot categories of direct action: P.G.D. and P.G.R.

But before we get there, some general comments:

First and foremost, and once and for all, let's quash the rumor that the more clothes you have, the longer you live. That's the bunk!

INCENTIVES to live long??? There are many. But what higher inducement than to outlive one's ugs? Outlive your ugs or your ugs will outlive you! In short: dress ugly now or dress it later—the choice is YOURS—but here's the kicker:

While an increased wearing of unfavored items will extend the life of the favored—and you surely have your work cut out for you—it would be a grave mistake to lose sight of the, uh, precariousness of your P-G predicament. Increased frequency ups other probabilities as well, including the prob of croaking while ug-attired. You may only be at the first fork in the geezer road, no further, and still it could hap any minute: you could die like a DAWG in that Disney World sweatshirt in what is it, ochre? mauve?, and be terminally known as one who *dressed repulsive*. It'll forever be your lot, your reputation, the final embarrassing entry in your GOOFUS FILE.

No, you'd be better served keeping it part-time. Designate a Pre-Geezer Day once, twice, three times a month. It would be helpful, natch, if Congress established it by statute—a *public* Pre-Geezer Day—but they haven't even legalized fucking yet . . . you can't depend on those stiffs. "Self help" (in the v. best sense) is what this is about: a P.G.D. of your very own— as personal as your P.I.N. Mark it on the calendar (don't forget!).

Every night, meanwhile, can be Pre-Geezer Night. Unless you've got a special date, wear your worst as pajamas or underjamas.

But even FOUR days a month might not shake a dent in your stash. You can't just *toss* unwanted wear'ems (didn't your mother tell you?)—you'll need a workable policy of P.G.R.: pre-geezer recycle.

And by recyc I don't mean pass 'em on. Don't think for a sec about inflicting your unwanteds on the clothesless! Would you give *tainted food* to the malnourished and starving? Would you have the homeless live in Port-A-Potties?

Your unsightly outfits are part of *your* karma; to pass them on is to bypass the hallowed ORDER OF THINGS. It is gar-batorially *invalid*, not to mention flat-out *rude*.

No—we're talking legitimate ALTERNATIVE USES here, not pass-alongs. A starting roster of justifiable recycs would include:

—Medical emergencies. Wrap a burn, bandage a bug bite, apply pressure where the roof of your mouth was gashed by broken glass in a tuna sandwich.

—Towels. With global warming, you may need sweat towels more than you currently 'spect. Be my guest: wipe your brow with the ugliest sock in the house.

—Curtains. For those sew inclined, a needle & thread will join up sundry g.g.'s (garish garments) real good. Too garish to wear on the street—but *dandy* cov'ring a window. When the sun comes shining thru, it's just like stained glass!

—Pillows. Geezers need naps. Fill one oversized shirt or t-shirt w/ seven others. How comfy!

—Speaking of naps: nappies. Washable, reusable monthly absorbers for those still menstruating, or f'r menstruating someones-U-know. Rig cut-to-fit apparel strips with tape or safety pins, or just stuff a handful in your undies. Never spend a DIME on napkins again!

—Hankies. Is there any real diff between noseblow on a pants leg and noseblow on an "official" handkerchief?

—Beverage enhancers. Shred 100% cotton-wear, plop in a blender w/ fruit juice or soy milk for a deelishus high-fiber drink. Chill in the icebox for healthful, flavorful popsicles . . . mmmm yum! First check labels to insure there is no polyester, nylon, rubber or fiberfill. (A fine use for rayon as well.)

—Shoes: bang nails with 'em. At least knock tacks in cork and particle board.

—Ties. *Ties??* What're you, some kind of fop? Ties you can just throw out.

A note on RAG CONVERSION. To gratuitously turn garments into rags before they *are* rags is for spudheads. If once in a longwhile you *need* a rag, that's one thing, but don't overdo it!

The byword in *any* act of recycle: to thine own geezer self be true. Be aboveboard in your search for alternatives—no arts & crafts for its own sake. That's for hobbyists, and dressing is hardly a hobby! An alt use should be as essential as an original one, i.e., the covering or adorning of human flesh in accordance with legal, practical, and esthetic conventions and pretensions.

Even if others don't know you've exceeded your sanction, *you* would know: you'd know you are a GEEZER AND A PHONY, and, well, they don't give out medals for THAT.

EPISTEMOLOGY

In days of yore, I was quasi-famed as a bloke fond of burning britches—pardon—bridges: torching them with extreme malice on the flimsiest of provocations.

If my age-peer crowd was once very hip to the activity, I was hipper. I gloried in it.

So how is it I'm not burning them TODAY?

Well, it isn't 'cause the onrush of years is starting to scare me; there are times lately where I'm scared shitless, but I can't say they've made me an advocate of bridge safety.

Nor am I refraining because I'm less of a firebug, or even 'cause there probably ain't too many *personal* bridges left to burn.

I simply can no longer TELL a bridge from the water— can't distinguish one from the other!—or dry fucking land. Or which end is "my" end. I wouldn't know how to *target* a bridge if you put a gun to my head.

Be that as it may, it's entirely possible I *am* in fact still burning th'm—burning 'em royally!—only I couldn't tell you with any certainty. Couldn't *begin* to guess the where and when.

THE COPENHAGEN STORY

I've never smoked cigarettes. There's supposedly some Russian doctor who says that if you're over 50 and have never smoked, go ahead—it's good for you. The nicotine will reju-venate a whole host of mental processes, it'll make you perky, on the ball, et cet., and since you're on in years, you most like-ly won't LIVE LONG ENOUGH to develop lung cancer. Sounds good—I *love* nicotine—but he's talking cigs, and I've never been able to get past the taste of the burning paper.

It's too bad I've instead used up (already!) my life quota of the form of tobacco I've gotten far & away the most mileage from: chew a/k/a chaw—my most odious intake at a time, like 20–25 years ago, when I really was something of a self-destructo.

And to boldly claim I ain't one still, well, that might ordinarily be the plan, but no sooner am I caught up in a writing project than old habits and old intakes walk right back and make their presence felt: cigars, rotten food, enough caffeine to stun a wildebeest. Beers? Not too many *while* writing, just as a "reward" for getting somewhere page-wise, and as the age count goes up, the page count goes down down *down*. Even short to medium things take long these days, leading to sieges like *this one* (six months! no end in sight!): a protracted rampage of screw-my-health, whatever it takes to crawl to the end.

Writing full tilt like I am, I can't bother with cooking—ya kidding?—so what I'm eating right now, my dinner!, is a jumbo bag of bar-b-q chips containing (let's see): sodium caseinate, sodium diacetate, disodium inosinate, disodium guanylate—a li'l bit o' sodium, huh?—in addition to salt and MSG. And food dyes, well, there are three yellows, a red, and two blues—BLUE?—if this was paint, you could do a fucking *seascape*. Which, take my word for it, I would not be eating if I weren't writing, and I wonder, d'you think (do ya do ya?) any of these ingredients could give you "C"?

'Cuz I do fear "C," okay?, and not simply on account of the little practice brush I've had with it (pinhead-size basal cell on my neck nine years ago). Every time I puff on a little-c

cigar and my heart races like Secretariat (so I know, inhale or
no, it's damnwell there in my SOMA), I'm all too conscious
of the "risk," and I thank my lucky STARS that a timely bum
experience ended my dance with the biggest and nastiest of
tobacco C's: Copenhagen. I gag just thinking about it . . .

Somewhere in the late '70s, when I was flirting with some
really yugsick chew-bacs like Red Man and Days Work, I saw
an ad in the back of *Sports Illustrated*—fill out this form and
Copenhagen ("the smokeless tobacco") will send you FOUR
free tins: what a deal. They weren't all Copenhagen *per se*—
there was also Skoal, and I vaguely remember a raspberry version of the same brown ammoniated stuff—but a tin wasn't
cheap, and their giving away so many should've made a ding-
dong firebell go off.

As it turned out, four was *exactly* enough to get me
hooked, *ooh* boy, and I mean DEPENDENT. Well, maybe not
textbook dependent—it wasn't like I needed it to get through
the hours, the day, or feel actual physical withdrawal pangs,
but I needed it for *fuck*sure to write. It was very speedy, and
right away. I could almost wake up on Copenhagen alone and
be writing, full throttle, immediately. My mind felt incredibly
mobile, darting back and forth, up and down, like a goddam
Pac-Man thingie . . . how remarkable. Once I realized its
effectiveness, how could I (why should I) stop?

For five years I used it every day, a "pinch between lip and
gum," refreshed and supplemented by mammoth fingerfuls as
required. Ammoniated? Dunno. But *something* caustic and
corrosive was part of the mix, 'cause in no time flat my inside
lip was being corroded. Eaten away. I'd go a week, two weeks,

corroding the right side, then switch to the left, and on and on back again, back again. Craters formed and healed, only to be dug anew. When I spit there would often be blood. Which told me pretty early on this was BAD JUJU—if it wasn't how you got cancer, there *was* no such animal. (This was before they painted chips blue.) Periodically, I would resolve to kick, I'd throw out my last tin, then as soon as I had to get a paragraph done right!now! I would run out and rummage through the dumpster . . . yowee.

What finally did it for me was one night I was at the typewriter, two teacups on my desk. One held cold tea, no milk, the other served as my spittoon. Two cups of dark brown liquid, and at some wee hour, bleary-eyed, I gulped down the cup of TOBACCO SPIT. I have not taken a pinch of C since.

RITES

When I was in high school, I didn't know anyone in a band. It was rumored that an original member of Jay & the Americans, someone not on any of their records, had once gone to our school—some blond guy a couple of classes ahead—but seeing his pic in a yearbook, I didn't recognize him.

The summer I was 20, a group of my friends formed a band, an imitation Rolling Stones, that played one chaotic bar date.

In '67, when I was 22, the "scene" mushroomed exponentially, and through my 20s I stood face to face with *hundreds* of people in bands, and was actual friends with several—I'd hate to call them celebs—known quantities of rock rock rock and roll.

By the time I was 32, I'd already been in two bands myself . . . big deal.

Today, membership in *at least one band*, however briefly, seems a rite of passage for practically everyone. How many people do you know, menwomen 30 and up, who've never been in a band, or tried to be in a band, or thought of learning bass because of an opening in some band that didn't care if their bassplayer could even *play*—they just needed somebody by Friday?

A rite, yes, and one that becomes more benign all the time—no longer on a par, as it once was, with selling dope or part-time whoring or joining the Marines.

Ironically or not (now that rock qua rock has ceased to be a bona fide universal solvent), in your average case it's more like a calisthenic, a strut . . . nothing wrong with that. The problem comes in when the calisthenic gets out of hand, starts calling for more and more reps, and lofty forethought or no, suddenly finds itself a MISSION.

FOLLY

I should talk about missions!

Fortunately or unfortunately, writing was not a rite of spring for me. It wasn't remotely anything I thought about as a kid, or an adolescent, or a postadolescent—it was one of the last things I'd ever 've wanted to grow up and do. I had no writing "heroes" whatsoever. I didn't like reading.

Yet at some point: BINGO. I was hooked.

Except for the ones I take in my mind, I haven't had a vacation in possibly 20 years, and I haven't taken too many weekends off in the last 30. If it's a day of the week, my nose is to the grindstone.

"Every day is Saturday," said Jack Kerouac and Handsome Dick Manitoba. For me, every day is more like Tuesday.

Which may be funny in a way, but I honestly don't always know what day it is in the "world out there." To occasionally be off by *one* day is understandable, but lately, with alarming regularity, I'm getting to be off by two or three.

There are times when I wish that a week as practiced by everyone else had only six days, or five . . . seven is just too many to keep track of.

THE GREAT JAZZ BOOK THAT ONLY I COULD WRITE

I'm not gonna write it.

USE

Biospherically speaking, as complexes of protoplasm, as machines operating at their uttermost efficiency, we humans have such pitifully limited use, and when our workings go a-clunker . . . phew!

When all we are is a pathetic waste of cells, how can you blame the directors of the factory for taking us out back and STEPPING ON US?

MODELS (2)

Harry Malfatti is the only guy I know with an eye patch. For a long while he didn't wear one. Though his left eye never looked where the right was looking, he never mentioned it—so you didn't either. Then one day, *voila!* "How do you like it?" he asked. "A present from Edna"—his 46-year-old sweety. "She thought it would make me look distinguished." Indeed: a distinguished, pony-tailed Captain Hook.

Harry is 63. A year ago, he quit his job as a dishwasher to work full-time on a book he'd been painstakingly researching, and slowly but surely pecking out, over nights and weekends of the previous 16 years. Before the dish gig, he worked as a Spanish professor, a library supervisor, assistant to a minor league hockey exec, until a wind-change convinced him *Enougha this white-collar b.s.!*—better to bus tables.

The first friend-o-mine living on Social Security, he opted to start collecting at 62, not 65, when he learned he'd have to live to 77 to come out ahead by waiting. "I'm crazy for long-shots, but that feels a smidge beyond my reach." Maybe, maybe not, but he does—*fuck* yes—expect to survive long enough to complete the book, and he's only on the first draft. The most singularly motivated buzzard I know, he'll let nothing stand in his way, including auto insurance. He's been driving uninsured for six months now, and is about to let the bank repossess his Nissan. "Sure I love driving places"—the track, for inst—"but there's NO TIME for it. All there's time for is the tome."

In addition to the staples of his diet, home-made goulash and saltines, he limits disbursement of his S.S. pittance to rent, laundry, gasoline (but not for long), cheap cigarettes, and bargain-basement beer, well, sometimes he'll splurge on Old Milwaukee.

Every few weeks, we get together at his pad and talk it up. He shows me some pages and I give him feedback and help copy-edit. I tell him what reads clunky or unclear, and I challenge and encourage him to *keep at it*. Since generally speaking I wouldn't advise my worst enemy to write, in current parlance I am his "enabler." All of which may seem even more unlikely when I tell you that the volume in progress is a work of ACADEMIC SCHOLARSHIP.

Y'might by now have a rough idea how I feel about academia—and academic writers—but Harry, though one serious prick, ain't one o' *them* in the slightest. Declaring himself an "academy of one"—a "*non*-spectator scholar"—he's taken on the task of composing a "secret intellectual history," one that crosses the bounds between shitloads of academic genres and sub-genres, and a sprinkling of non-acs as well. Even that may sound like standard fare—what the hey—but I've read most of the damn thing, and it's often *terrific*.

And how is it terrific? Well, for one thing, it is really *all over the place*. I've seen 300 pages, sardine-packed with references to hotsos from Herodotus to Sappho to Boethius to Bernard of Clairvaux to Cervantes to Voltaire to Ludwig Feuerbach to Sacher-Masoch to William James to Giuseppe Verdi to Alfred Jarry to Babe Ruth to Joseph Campbell to Robert Mapplethorpe to Rasputin to Max Weber to Lash La Rue (I kid you not) to Edna St. Vincent Millay to Edna Vitaliano, Harry's womanfriend—a former underwear model. "I'd like to also have her on the cover"—he winks, showing me the pic he has in mind . . . ah *ha*.

All over, that's one, and for another—hey—it's a big, sprawling, jolly mess of SMUT.

The Chi-Psi-Omega Hypothesis: The Search for a Collective Pornography—that's the working title. Harry cautions me, however, about labeling it smut. "Don't get carried away. 'Pornography' is just a buzz-word to pique the reader's interest. Yes, by all means, I'm concerned with the evolution of sexual thinking, that is, *human* sexual thinking, and from what you've read so far, you know that on an anthropological—scratch that—on a *zoological* level, we as a species have a neocortex—do we ever!—but do the dendrites in our genitalia perform a less libidinal function than those in the genitalia of goats?

"And therefore?? Well, I could just as easily have subtitled it *The Continental Divide Between Inorganic and Organic Thinking* . . . an allusion to a prevalent dogma among *professional* academy thinkers. All I'm trying in my humble way to do is *undivide things a little*." He shoots me a stern look, then winks. "Smut! You're absolutely right! I like it!"

There are times when I worry about my friend's health. Though he hasn't seen a doctor in years, he swears his heart, liver and lungs are "not half bad, well, not three-quarters." A few months ago, when a strange tingling sensation visited both forearms up to the elbow, he refused medical attention. "It isn't really that unpleasant," he insisted. Although not knowing what was going on was unnerving, the worst part, before it subsided, was losing a week's work. "Time ain't on my side, Jack! I need every last nanosecond."

Pop another Ol' Milwaukee!

IRRELEVANT

A simultaneous mass exit, like the whole world going down in one fell swoop—"armageddon," "holocaust," "nuke time U.S.A.," whatever you wanna call it—is terrifying in no small part because it would make all of our individual deaths irrelevant, rob them of their uniqueness—a bogus uniqueness, to be sure, but one forever seen as crucial to the projected end gestalt. (You're born alone, you die alone—*that* old chestnut.)

"See here how everything lead up to this day," sang the Grateful Dead in 1970, speaking of an old man's day of dying, his lying in pain (for passersby's amusement) as his sole final anything. With world snuffout, personal agony has no moment, and nobody lies dying, everybody just DIES . . . ceases to be . . . is and then summarily ISN'T . . . and nothing else is, or was, ever again, ever . . . even words aren't, and weren't.

The thought of dying young—"before your time"—in such a universal termination is one grimly unacceptable excruciation. To be over 45, let's say, or 50—to already be in the "death zone"—and be faced with imagining that same annihilation is quite another. To have toiled and moiled through a lifesworth of delusions, for an approximate-minimum full-life's duration, and have it add in a flash to undifferentiated molecules on the slag heap of undifferentiated nothing—now THAT is a frightening outcome to grapple with.

If for no other reason than to serve as an exemplar, let me get fatuously personal: to be forced to surrender the concept of FUTURE, and of strangers not yet born, their *grandparents* not yet born, finding delight (or finding anything) in my silly writings; to in the same breath abandon, after so long and foolishly embracing, something as absurd as the notion of works (and words!) that OUTLIVE MEN . . . well . . . fuck shit piss godfuckingdammit . . . *tell me about it*, okay?

UNFINISHED BUSINESS

I should *probably* take acid at least one more time.

NOSTALGIA

In Guided by Voices' "Have It Again," Robert Pollard poses the question "What would you give to be 9 or 10 again?," then

the same Q re "19 or 20," and finally "49 or 50" . . . oh, price-
less yrs! oh, precious past!

Yeah, yeah . . . *right*.

Y'gotta believe me when I tell you I wouldn't wanna have
it, and would hate to *have* to have it—to be any of those
ages!—again. They all have their work and their woe, and the
work and the woe outweigh the jollity and the joy.

Sheezus—I *pity* the poor 19-yr-old stuck living NOW—on
this planet—why the hell would I wanna be one? Nor would
I 'zactly wanna revisit being one THEN.

To get there from *here* would mean toting a 12-pack
(min.) of, oh, call it insight—you can't not bring it.
Perspicacity? Or worse: a small working replica of my current
late-model shit detector—a laptop s.d., if you will. You would
only hafta crank it halfway for it to do its dirtywork. Which
on time-trip turf would bring out some of my more
GEEZERESQUE TRAITS, like my stick-in-the-mud tenacity
at "seeing through shucks" (oh yawn). The balmy things we
oldtimers take pride in!

Now of course I wouldn't mind being younger in body,
you betcha—but a younger, less up-to-speed *psyche*? No
thankyou! Innocence, relative or otherwise, is really not something I would care to recapture. As it is, I'm still a fairly innocent schmuck, and it wouldn't appeal to me t' be MORE
SO—certainly not at the expense of all the oceans of sweat
I've bled getting to "know better," becoming even marginally
less of a dumb-ass fuck.

If innocence, or non-disbelief, emotional benightedness,
whatever, be the key ingredient in getting off on a full range

of hands-as-dealt, well, that's completely, totally objection-able. There might well be more pleasure, and hotter and cool-er kicks, to be had being more-dumb as opposed to less-dumb, but at this advanced date, something in the emotional ecolo-gy of the situation disposes me towards the latter . . . and if that makes me an old fussbudget, hey, so be it.

It takes all (as they say) kinds.

John Cassavetes once said: "There are no great films . . . only great scenes." Well, I'm not sure I even *do* miss all that much about any o' these old temporal turfs, epochs of ancient self, even from AFAR, but yes (ah *me*): there were certainly moments!

HAIKU #3

does my dick have scales?
(many miles since last checkup)
rust or barnacles?

AGO

With the triumph of the CD now complete, none of this has much currency anymore, but it once was a semi-big deal to reach a record-speed milestone in one's own life—to turn 33–1/3, for example. Though it hardly meant as much as turning 30, 40, or 20, it was something you were sure to be aware of; it was good for a giggle.

By the time I turned 45 it no longer meant *zip* in the contempo promenade; and if I make it to 78, whether or not I still have my wits about me, I don't anticipate even thinking about it.

Hey—I'm already at an age where I can look back on major occurrences of my life, of my *adult* life, that happened 33–1/3 years AGO.

Before my next birthday, in fact, it will be 33–1/3 since the release of my all-time favorite 33–1/3'er, *The Beatles* (a/k/a "The White Album"), and one of the most happily recalled nights of my life.

One Friday afternoon, November '68, the FM affiliate of WABC, New York, announced that "the new Beatle album" would be played in its entirety that evening. This was at a time when it wasn't even for sure there would *be* another Beatle album. (Their previous LP, *Magical Mystery Tour*, hadn't really been an album at all. True, it contained the A and B sides of some great singles, but the new stuff, what little there was of it, included arguably their worst cut ever, "Your Mother Should Know.")

An actual new album, and a *double* album yet: yay! At the Long Island home of a band called the Soft White Underbelly, with whom I was living off and on, aiding and abetting and writing lyrics, everybody was STOKED.

As zero hour approached, we smoked some very potent hash and ordered a pizza. We: the band, my girlfriend Roni and I, the drummer's girlfriend Helen. I don't remember Eric ("Manny"), the soon-to-be singer, being there. Les, the vocalist of record (who still lived in the house and was all but ignored), definitely wasn't, but all the others were: Albert, Allen, Andy, Don. That night, we would be something very-much like "family," or "tribe"—oh, even "household" would do—in that Late Sixties maxi-kinship sense—though no such unanimity of connection would ever come close to rearing its head again.

Bob Lewis, one of the more bearable, and less hyper-obnoxious, deejays in New York, began by announcing: "First I'm gonna skip around and play things in a sequence that means something to *me*. Then I'll play the whole album in the right order." Twice!!

Beginning with "Bungalow Bill," we heard cut after cut of what the Beatles at their best always *did* best—an ur-rendition of Hybrid Music in extremis: "Back in the U.S.S.R." (the Velvet Underground meets the Beach Boys, overseen by their common ancestor Chuck Berry) . . . "Sexy Sadie" (doo wop meets diva madness) . . . "While My Guitar Gently Weeps" (the Beau Brummels do "Greensleeves") . . . "Long, Long, Long" (the Byrds' "Get to You" as rethought by Procol Harum) . . . "Helter Skelter" (Larry Williams visits Dion & the Belmonts' "I Can't Go On, Rosalie," with bumpkinized Jimi Hendrix accompaniment). Having musically stripmined so mega-much terrestrial acreage, was there anything left for the MopTops to mine but the sky?

We flashed insane grins and shook our heads, muttering WOW after WOW. To call the experience "religious" is to understate the awe we felt in witnessing the most cornucopially profuse, most abundantly generous band rock-roll had known, all but given up for dead, suddenly returning with its greatest and most bountiful work. When the bogue-Caribbean "Ob-La-Di, Ob-La-Da" came on, we rose as one, danced round the room and hugged each other.

After the second play of "Good Night," Ringo's neo-Mantovani masterpiece, we scampered out into the cold, high on more than the hash, and kicked up our heels, feeling (for prob'ly the final time in the Sixties . . . or ever) a distinct sense of UNLIMITED POSSIBILITY. Even Allen, a mocker who until then hadn't even liked the Beatles, was driven to say, "Well, I guess the object is no longer just to listen, or even memorize—it's for everybody to internalize this shit and SPEAK IT."

We taped the whole thing on an old reel-to-reel recorder. When I woke the next morning, Don, who when the band became Blue Öyster Cult would be known as Buck Dharma (little mister Heavy Metal!), was rewinding and playing a portion of the tape, trying to learn the chords to, of all things, "Mother Nature's Son," playing them back on his guitar. What a beautiful little coda to the occasion . . . event . . . happening.

(That's right: an Old War Story. If the world ends tomorrow, at least I've taken one last hike through it.)

THE JOHNNY STOMPANATO FAN CLUB

poor sad
bo
zos
I feel

soooooo
bad
for all the Bobs,
Robs, Randys, Mandys,
Maggies, marrieds, Marys,
Garys, Gabbys, crabbies,
Babses, Sabus and Beaus
as they all

LOVE
one another

AND

die

GEEZER MUSIC

• Joe Callicott, "Fare You Well Baby Blues" (on *Mississippi Delta Blues, Vol. 2*, Arhoolie CD 402)

• Skip James, "I'm So Glad" (on *She Lyin'*, Edsel EDCD 379)

• Coleman Hawkins, "Time on My Hands" (on *Sirius*, Pablo/Original Jazz Classics OJCCD–861–2)

In early 1930, after cutting two sides—a 78—including the kiss-off classic "Fare Thee Well Blues," Joe Callicott returned to a life of sharecropping punctuated by appearances at

Mississippi fish fries and, occasionally, Memphis frolics, not recording again for 37 years.

By then he'd missed out on the "country blues revival" (culminating, for better and worse, in the 1964 Newport Folk Festival), during which a number of long-forgotten blues players were exhumed as "folk artists" by entrepreneurs of varying exploitational bents. Not on the "A" list of targeted "rediscoveries," Callicott had to wait until the summer of '67, when he was 65, to record nine songs, six of them released while he was alive, most notably a remake of "Fare Thee Well," this time entitled "Fare You Well Baby Blues."

Slower than the original, its picking less nimble, it's nonetheless a v. passable account of the tune. A snatch of old lyric is dropped ("You got more men than a two-ton truck can haul") and a new line added ("What is you gonna do when your trouble get like mine?"), but the vocal is every bit as strong, with the identical balance of anguish and resignation. There would be no further recordings, and between two and four years later Callicott was no more. (So relatively insignificant was he to even his rediscoverers—and their "folklorist" compeers—that nobody kept close enough tabs on him to know with any accuracy when he died.)

An "A"-lister all the way—he'd cut 18 sides in 1931 (including two—"22–20 Blues" and "Devil Got My Woman"—commonly assumed to have influenced the young Robert Johnson)—the 62-year-old Skip James was one of a dozen-plus bluesmen to play Newport '64, which afforded him access to what biographer Stephen Calt has called "the dreary coffeehouse circuit." It also led to Cream's recording of

James's "I'm So Glad," which earned him a larger fistful of coins than sales of his own two albums for Vanguard . . . the royalties from ALL of which would be devoured by his final hospitalization with cancer (ain't life sublime?).

Four weeks after Newport, just before his body started hurtling down the drain, he recorded the first post-'31 version of "I'm So Glad," and probably the best. (Though superior to the Vanguard take of '65, it would not be released until '93, when he was already dead 24 years.) His guitar work is no great shakes, but he sings some really impassioned shit, max-ing out the misery, the distress, in the *non*-falsetto parts, near-ly reversing the intensity flow of the '31 original—no mean feat. Has there ever been a performance of a song, any genre, more ABOUT (and from) exhaustion and confusion? (What a thoroughly worldbeaten guy.) And hey, don't "sad" and "mad" rhyme with "glad"? While emotionally scattered, the original had *some* gladness—this has NONE.

Adolphe Sax, a Belgian, created prototypes of the various members of the saxophone family somewhere around 1840, but it wasn't until the second and third decades of the 20th century that anyone anywhere would figure out how to play more than imitation animal sounds, and other comedic "cir-cus" effects, on a single one of them. Somewhere before 1920, New Orleans jazzman Sidney Bechet performed the deed on soprano sax, followed in the '20s proper by Coleman Hawkins on tenor.

For the next 40 years, Hawkins would be known for a sen-suous (often dangerous) muscularity of tone and phrase, a signature warmth emanating from the chest and belly. He had a "sense of the ballad" as advanced, and as simple, as any horn-player's ever, and was a majestic improviser. According to lore, he was the chronological FIRST to "tell a story" on a saxophone, and as time went by the stories got longer and more intricate. (Check the '39 "Body and Soul," the '45 "Talk of the Town," the '48 "Picasso.")

In 1966, at his last studio session, the phrases at his command for storying are fairly short and unmenacing, and not always perfectly formed (or even sturdy), and they end as often as not with an almost gauzy vibrato like that favored by his acolyte and rival Ben Webster. You can just about hear columns of toneless, pitchless air vibrating, and ceasing to vibrate . . . sound unto silence.

A minute and a half into "Time on My Hands," the rhythm section drops out, and for the next two minutes–plus, which feel to the listener like five or six or ten—time as *perceived* being so palpably molded, so altered—the 62-year-old Hawk delivers not so much a story as a valediction. So little breathing time remains, yet time is *his* . . . micro-duration is macro . . . all time is NOW. It's not always such a great idea to lean heavily on metaphors, but astro-time implodes, matter too, and Sirius, brightest star in the heavens, becomes a neutron star . . . a campfire . . . a matchbook aflame in a skeleton hand. All entropy, all destiny compress the final recitation to a throaty whimper . . . a final peep.

A poignantly MAGNIFICENT peep, but a peep . . . then neverending stillness.

L 15

Nothing I write—no sustained *episode* of writing—feels like a winning fight anymore. 15-rounders, all of 'em, and the best I ever do is lose by a split decision.

Sometimes one judge will score it for me by a point or two, if only because he remembers when I had all the moves—and still digs seeing them in flashes—even though they're only simulations now. I shrug when they read his scorecard 'cause I know it's just old sentiment speaking. (If you're not up on these things, I was once a cross between Willie Pep and Cleveland Williams.)

The worst thing about it is I never get KO'ed. It would be a lot healthier: fewer overall punches taken, fewer eyes swoll shut and noses broken, fewer witless displays of "courage" trapped on the ropes before miraculously clinching. Seems like 20 years since a ref last stepped in and stopped it.

Ooh my soul, do I wish I could fight a 4-round prelim once in a while.

With every sigh, every sneeze, I feel every body shot I've ever taken.

ALWAYS

I always stoop down to pick up worms after rain or the runoff from watering lawns or washing cars has trapped them squirming on the pavement, unable to make it back to safe sod whence they came. If they show any signs of life, I move them to a patch of dirt or grass or a cozy heap of wet news-papers . . . anywhere there's less chance of them being stepped on or dried up by the onslaught of sun.

For as long as I can remember I've done this, and I'm confident I always will.

IMPORTANT

At this late stage of things, all previous statements aside, it's important to me that I continue to write for one reason alone: BECAUSE IT'S ALL I KNOW. So important is it that if it should kill me, well, that would be OK, at least as caus-es-o-death go . . . as long, that is, as I've *finished* whatever I was writing in the process.

Writing has micro-squat to do anymore with "glory" or "craft" or "expression"—none of those are even elements. It's simply SOMETHING THAT MUST BE DONE, again and again and again, to certain vocational and avocational specifi-cations, something no more significant in and of itself than brushing my teeth, or shopping for groceries, or changing a light bulb . . . a *grander* version of those things, perhaps, but really only the *eensiest* jot less prosaic an ACTIVITY.

Whether being so fixated, so hooked, on something so wearing and tearing—and at the same time so intrinsically not-much—constitutes a good habit or a bad habit is of no concern to me, though I'll concede that "objectively" it's prob'ly a ver-rry bad habit (worse than Copenhagen!) . . . 's merely *my* habit. My filthy, dirty, bloody TERMINAL CALLING.

SOMEBODY'S FAVORITE SONG, EVER

The Del-Vikings' "Come Go with Me."

COMPLETE

Image of a tombstone on my left forearm: I'm now complete. Tattoo for each forearm, one for each shoulder—complete for now. A finite, if prolonged, work in progress, begun 8/69, finished 10/99. Should a falling piano land on my head, I'm set.

If only in this one regard, right now I feel something quite-like peace—and a sense of life-mission accomplished—far more than if I'd had another ten books published. As Hegel said somewhere down the line, the Absolute unfolds itself—and all my writing put together, Absolutely, as both mission and accomplishment, becomes as nothing beside my four tattoos in equilibrium.

Since I drilled none of these into my skin, nor did more than suggest slight changes in the design of a couple (a nail-polished hand reaching upward from foliage beside the stone; full genital peek-a-boo for "Ruby," babe-in-residence on my right shoulder), I'm more their canvas than contriver, their consumer than author, yet they comprise the sole body of work I will take, literally, to the grave with me.

For the moment now my body, as home, as baggage, as tabula no-longer-rasa, feels stable, and I feel whole and undivided. This will change soon enough, when the death of my cat impels me to have his likeness, or some generic cat-face w/ teeth fiercely bared, drawn and drilled on my *inner* right fore-arm, thus requiring a symmetrical follow-up *toot sweet* . . . before, anyhow, the baby grand flattens me.

Symmetry . . . *sheez.*

Now that I'm no longer a Platonist, nor any kind of monist or especially an idealist, I wonder: why does such hoohah obsess me?

FOREVER

I absoposilutely do *not* wanna live forever.

If I somehow got to live a THOUSAND TIMES, ha, it'd take some weird, unforeseeable lunacy (at age 56 and up) to make me fantasize stretching it even ONCE beyond the bounds of a single lifetime, a time-coded unit existence.

THE ATTICS OF MY LIFE

I've lived in plenty of buildings with basements, but I've never had an attic.

Back when I was a really, really, really stupid kid, long before I ever got laid, I used to dream of kissing a girl, on the lips but dryly, in an attic.

The first gal with whom I had even rudimentary sex, and would go on to have full-boogie intercourse, invited me to play with her one afternoon, while her parents watched TV, up in her suburban attic. It was summer, and so hot it made *perfect* sense to take our pants off, and she let me finger her, but she wouldn't let me stick my finger in . . . that other place.

Have I given this torrid day a moment's thought since? Why do I now?

"THE GOOD FIGHT"

All good fights, so-called—"gallant endeavors"—are good or gallant only as long as you want to endure them, as long as you in some sense *enjoy fighting and/or endeavoring*. Once the whambang ritual itself gets to be superfluous or pointless or exorbitant, it becomes a futile waste of breath like any other . . . a bullshit masochistic RIFF . . . a birthday-suited chump's aerobic convulsion. Nobody needs more scar tissue.

Well, maybe scarification artists need it, but the universe doesn't need one more work of high-booty art, or one more conscientious artist.

UNFINISHED PLAY
SCENE ONE

JOSETTE. Pass the potatoes.
LOOOOIE. Yeah, sure.
JOSETTE. . . . . . (*Glares at Looooie.*)
LOOOOIE. Fuck you.

SCENE TWO

JOSETTE. You're a big fucking dope.

LOOOOIE. *You're* a pig-fucking dope.

JOSETTE. I said "big fucking dope."

LOOOOIE. You're that too.

JOSETTE. Actually, you *are* a pig-fucking dope.

SCENE THREE

A large clear-glass bowl of potato salad on

LAST WILL 'N' TEST

if the flies want me
let the flies have me
if I stink too bad
take drastic action

SICK PERSON'S CAR

sick person's car
is a car parked where there's no parking tuesday
& it's thursday & the ticket is still on the windshield

or maybe it's a dead person's car

STAN STASIAK: DEAD MAN

As things got underway the rose-covered casket was closed. Knowing how big Stan "The Man" Stasiak had been in life, I didn't think it was long enough—had they folded him at the knees? Sad large men, some with families, more with bizarre hairpieces and dyejobs, all but filled the pews of St. Johns Funeral Home, Portland, OR. Must've been 100, 125 in the room, but when the minister asked for friends of Stan to verbally, y'know, *honor* the sonofagun—tell his tale—only two came forward. "He was," said the first, "a gentle giant" who in his final years had "walked with God." With great conviction he offered that Stan was now in "a better place than we are"— pointing upward—as opposed to simply being nowhere, which is always (some would argue) a better place than most. The other stated merely that Stan was "one of the best."

Neither made reference to what a dirty, rotten bastard he'd been in the ring—well, *some* rings—notably Madison Square Garden, where in the early '70s he reigned as *the* abysmal brute. A magnificent snarling overweight fuck with ugly side-burns like late-period Elvis, he was a bad guy's bad guy when bad guys were the only thing interesting about wrestling.

Them and their managers, and Stan had one of the finest (second only to Freddie Blassie): the Grand Wizard. Barked the Wizard when his charge took the title belt from Pedro Morales: "We'll have to steam-clean it for seven hours to remove the stink of garlic" . . . like wow.

Stan's signature stroke, the dread heart punch, one of the hokiest finishing moves of the era, was a bareknuckle right telegraphed for miles and uncorked at the vague vicinity of his opponent's chest. Once it landed, there was no getting up—call the medics, get the stretcher (which Stan would promptly kick). At their utter utmost, his hi-jinks embodied the total bathos of it all: the apogee of low—as abysmally bozo as brute. (And don't think I mean these things "negatively.")

Prob'ly the only jerk in the house who'd seen him do his thing while headlining the Garden (before full houses— 21,000—who hated his guts), I thought for a moment to get up and tell it. When the moment passed, the minister blandly resumed his generic bereavement rap, filling time with lines off a sheet supplied by surviving Stasiaks, telling us that Stan had been an orphan, that he'd played hockey and met celebrities like Burl Ives, Moe of the Three Stooges, Morey Amsterdam and (last but not least) JFK. A generic funeral, a dismal affair . . . the nullification of a life rather than its celebration . . . final nail in the coffin . . . and then!

Grey grey grey grey GREY . . . to call it simply grey is to shortchange the radiance, the aura emanating from the suddenly open casket, from the six-day-old corpse of 60-year-old Stan Stasiak. His hair was white-grey, his face was grey-grey

. . . ash-grey, soot-grey mammal meat. I didn't go to 'Nam, so I never saw anyone look so dead—not personally, not even in movies (Martin Landau as the *dead* Lugosi in *Ed Wood* was lively by comparison). It was Wednesday, he'd died the previous Thursday, and this was the best the cosmeticians could pull off (oh! to have seen th' meat before they went to work). It would not be easy on real-time individual initiative (e.g., smoking/drinking/drugging, intake of cholesterol, carcinogens, etc.) (as opposed to hit by an asteroid, locked overnight in a pizza oven, shot 20 times in the face) to DO DEAD an iota better than Stan.

In a Schopenhauerian world-as-will-and-idea sense, it's highly implausible that back when it mattered, in his wildest dreams of what it all might conceivably have meant, he could've imagined the sheer devastation of his creation made FLESH—an ACTUAL heart punch!—nor could he have fancied that receiving one someday himself (cause-o-death: congestive heart failure) would be one of his greatest achievements. (This is not like Roy Cohn getting AIDS, for inst; it's like Thor getting hammered, or Guillotine being guillotined—which I believe did happen.)

SCREAM IT FROM MOUNTAINS that Stan Stasiak was a goddam *monster*—a champeen and then some—when it came to getting deathed!

THE LIFE OF CHRIST
(DECEASED)

I'm about
six inches tall
and I punch
silly-looking leather things

DUST

brown 'n' sugar
sugar gold
Sugar PANTS!
— "Smellin' with Helen" (1968)

Twenty-five years ago, before many of you kiddies were born, I slipped the sausage to Helen Wheels, who died last week. It's possible (tho how could we be certain?) she's the first woman I've fucked to end up dead. There's one I once poked who went on to rip her eyes out, or so she later said—grabbed hold, she claimed (first one, then the other), and yanked 'em—but being blind isn't quite the same as being NOTHING.

When I first met her, in 1967 or early '68, Helen Robbins, as she then was known, was a shy little college girl, sweetheart of the drummer for this band called Soft White Underbelly. When I say *little* I simply mean she was on the small side, short, and the median height of the band, as bands go, was itself below average—a buncha peewees. (Near that median myself, I tend to notice these things.) Short and cute, on the cusp (at least) of pretty, tho by no means beautiful, "sexy" in a nonspecific way, a warm if not hot mammal heat source, an appealing soft creature, about 18, casually groomed, a very sweet smile when she smiled, but above all shy . . . reticent . . . she didn't say very much at all.

If in certain lights, on a cursory scan, her casualness might've passed for that of a "hippie chick," there was nothing especially hippie about her in either a kosmic or style-sheet sense, nor was there anything all that radical-lifestyle about the band, whose music was more psychedelic than they were (just as later, in their Blue Öyster Cult incarnation, their music would be more *metal* than they purported to be), whose preferred drug was probably beer, who would bicker over who was gonna buy the next round of peanut butter: just a pack of *kids*, more unhip than hip, kids "too nice" (maybe) for the long haul of rock and roll.

In the dump they rented in mid-'68, four decaying floors on a Long Island street where Gatsby might've boogied Daisy whatserface in 1923, a place I called home for most of a year, Helen (generous, cheerful, more outgoing, still very sweet) became a source of stability and continuity. She and Albert the drummer were kinda cute together, like R. Crumb's adorable Bearzy-Wearzies, and their room, neatest in the house, was the one chosen by Walrus, the household's favorite cat, to have her kittens. (Providing equal succor to the least favored, whenever she felt entitled to a "wish" she reserved it for Tiger, an old beat-up tomcat stray whose tail had gone numb.)

A knock at the door one night in late '69 altered the sweetness of the picture. Without prelude, a couple in their early 20s, total strangers, asked, "Where's the mescaline?" It turned out Helen, without consulting anyone, had set up a little business. For customers she'd suss out the younger patrons of the liquor store she sometimes worked—"If you like gin, I know something that'll *really* get you high."

A fucking wave of panic swept the house. Rich people, straight people, lived next door and across the way, like this ad exec in A.A. whose accounts included Kiku cologne—*the* upscale male stinkum of its time—and who didn't cotton to his mid-teen son hanging out with a goddam rock band in the first place. It was, no shit, a somewhat dangerous neighborhood to be dealing drugs to strangers. For weeks, every time we heard a siren in the distance, all of us, Helen included, would stop dead in our tracks, figuring *this was it*. (Lock us up, throw 'way the key.)

Next to kick in was Helen's SLUT PHASE. I was gone by then, sorry I missed it, but tales traveled far & wide of her spreading for anyone who walked in the door, including this big ogre named Monty who used to lurk about in a fringe jacket and—I vaguely recall—a knife on his belt . . .

And THEN: Fall of the House of Underbelly. While the band was in L.A. recording an album that would never come out, she took too much acid, failed to get oil for the heater, and the pipes froze and burst, flooding the house, revivifying two years' worth of dried catshit, causing mold to sprout everywhere. In the dead of winter this is what they returned to. By summer she was G-G-GONE.

*   *   *

Time, as it commonly does, lurches on. Years pass.

From out of the blue Helen would phone me, or I'd run into her at BÖC shows or here and there in Manhattan. Small talk, how's tricks, not exactly flirtation but *almost*. She had the same lovely smile. Finally, 1975, I'm about to leave New York, now's my chance. I call—hi howzit?—go over to her Lower East Side pad with a pint of Myers rum.

Her cunt was tight, or tight enough. Small is good for some things—eminently practical things—after all. After we'd fucked three times, she whispered, "Eat me and I'll come again" . . . how nice. There was a lot of bounce, sauce and sass, a lot of enthusiasm, even if it wasn't quite rapture or fire-works. No fuss, no muss—the closest I came, in my waning days in the Apple, to boogie w/out courtship, fanfare or grief. In the decades since, I've almost never beat off thinking about her, but yes, it *was* nice.

For a couple years we stayed in touch. Now officially Miz Wheels, she formed a band and recorded for cheezy little labels like Real American Records . . . flags all over the place . . . stickers on the cover, "Guaranteed 100% American Music" . . . oh boy. In publicity shots she's a sawed-off Lily Tomlin, which is not to say she looks dyke-y, she just looks hard, stern, "handsome" rather than cute, more like a racehorse (or pray-ing mantis) than a bearzy-wearzy. Lots of metal and leather.

The letters, once long, got short: "Hi! Do they play my record where you are? Me & my old man got a tarantula, 4 snakes & a 1930 Harley Davidson! Hope you're fine too!" "Rock and Roll Made a Man Out of Me" sang Handsome Dick Manitoba, vocalist for the band which for a time backed her up; well it made *something* out of Helen as well. It got her to the fucking door, and on the other side was NOT MUCH.

By no stretch of the imagination was her music—or its "attitude"—Punk, as was occasionally claimed. (Punk wouldn't even *piss* on the flags.) Altho possibly more hard-edged—"tough"—"kick-ass"—than any Underbelly install-ment's would ever be, it was just basically the kind of rock that celebrates nothing real (not for anybody with half a brain, 2/5 of a heart), that is so lowest-common-denom *by design* that the LEAST toxic thing it's gonna do is make you stupid. (The kind that most working bands, American or oth-erwise, continue to produce, with or without trying.)

Slightly later, Helen took up bodybuilding, which led, sup-posedly, to bit parts in some movies. Her only listing in the Internet Movie Database *is Toxic Avenger, Part II* (1989), as the fifth of five "Bad Girls."

A few months ago I had my hemorrhoids removed and spent two days in the hospital, living to talk about it. In a dif-ferent clinic the other day, Helen had her back fussed with and didn't make it. Two optional surgeries. One lives, one dies. Dust.

But first: wormfood.

The wage of Sin is death.

The wage of Rock is death.

The wage of everything is death. It's simply the end towards which all meat properly TENDS.

Dig it.

MINUS FIVE AND COUNTING

for Richard Grossman

O_2 tube in nostrils
earphones in ears
air conditioner: on
(the weather is a bitch)
fluid-bloated hippo legs up 1 . . . 2 on a towel-covered chair
theme song from *Rockford*
BLAST OFF
and in 5 minutes
asleep
(and in 5 days you'll be dead)

neck bent
like a twig about to snap
face not at
peace
pillow falling
things falling
bottles falling

bottles breaking
thick green
or blue glass
but no glass

not a sound

THE WISDOM IN OUR UNDERWEAR: FINAL NOTES ON THE ONLY CENTURY WE'VE GOT FOR ANOTHER WEEK

MY CENTURY, YOUR CENTURY, BOBO OLSON'S CENTURY

> Century's short
> but centuries long
> should be
>
> limited.
>
> —"Microwave,"
> William Carlos Williams

It ended abruptly around 1970, or slightly earlier. '69 would be a good likely date. If you were born after that and care about such biz, too bad—and too bad, yes, 'cause it *is* too bad—but everything since then has just been Out There somewhere, off the frigging Map. After the century and its representatives tossed it all away.

The century where it all went to hell—but WHAT went to hell?

Where the means were found to sweep all wisdom, all true sass, and most (if not quite literally *all*) beauty under the rug, to brush it off humankind's underwear.

Where the distance between the real and the acceptably fake narrowed and narrowed to functional insignificance.

New new NEW, lotsa freaking N*E*W, but ultimately (and merely): new bread, new circuses, new repression.

But nothing as *utterly* new, as new w/out historical precedent, as terminal closure. Termination 4-ever. Although Burroughs used to claim it closed, ending all real earthly Possibility, in the *18th* century. Or was it the 17th? Dunno. (You could ask him if he wuzn't dead.)

So many, so-o-o many things happening only to unhappen; to be trivialized and marginalized by failure, success, and the oversight of Crowd Control Central (which you bet your *ass* exists); to undercut their own being, deflavor and denature their own act, to wet-tissue-paper nullity. And I ain't just talking rock and uh ROLL . . .

On the shortlist of things/lost, or even not-lost (and possibly lookin' quite healthy), but still d-d-DONE:

The NF fucking L (NB fucking A) (March—ha ha ha—Madness).

Boxing as an event staged in venues other than cow pastures.

Wrestling, for crying out loud.

Hollywood, anyone? (Independent cinema, ditto.)

Did I hear the word "journalism"?

TV. TV? Tee *vee*??

Democracy as even a phantom cliché tendered as a sop to rubes (*still* the major mega-demographic).

Cultural liberation. Sexual freedom. Civil, y'know, rights. Public . . . what was it? . . . education.

Anybody in the house remember graduated income tax?

Watergate, by golly. What'd it lead to besides Nixon being SAINTED? (Century of the Bully.)

Marx proven right! And right ON! Again and again and AGAIN! (You bet your *mom's* rosy ass he was.)

Capitalism (which in endgame = Hedonism) and Puritanism: two nasty trains, always running, but now running in sync: the scare of nastier, more existentially calamitous mortifications (like another Depression, or nuclear 'radication, or no more dirty mags) to keep us neurotic, force us to settle for less dire plights and lower-yield varieties of (ever more expensive) symptomatic relief.

Kicks??? A concept nuked back to the Stone Age; a shell game, at best, translucent as a broken bay window.

A century in which some *odd* couplings have occurred, where (for most intents and many purposes) a familiar face named Jesus, for inst, got mated with this new guy named Hitler, yielding one awesome composite force, a unitary "belief" generatrix for some kazillion-plus population units . . . something t' do with racism . . . discipline . . . robotic obedience . . . and of course Clean Living. (Is anyone paying attention?)

It was the best of shit.

It was the worst of shit.

It was the best of shit.
It was the worst of shit.
It is the worst of shit.
It's the shitttttttttttttttt.
(Forever.)

PROPHECY AND POSTPHECY

"2000 Man"—who'd have thunk it?

What seemed at the time like a bit of comic relief, a topical joke on side one of *Their Satanic Majesties Request*, the Rolling Stones' entry (11/67) in the *Sgt. Pepper* overproduction sweepstakes, now reads like one of the great, and maybe the *last* great, documents of future-think.

"My name is a number, a piece of plastic film" . . . "I am having an affair with a random computer" . . . even a dose of multi*planetary* multiculturalism: "Oh Daddy, proud of your planet; oh Mommy, proud of your sun"—how's *that* for prescience?

Who'd've thought such a *lampoon* of future-think would come to pass so quickly, so thoroughly—or was it a truism even then?—and nobody'd even be snickering?

And that other more-than-date: 1984.

By which time, compared to the hand history had actually dealt, "1984" (the concept) had become a mild little what-are-you-complaining-about?, the Orwell vision having been superseded by something far more weasely and malevolent.

Big Mean Uncle certainly did watch you, but more than that you were watching *him* (his 8-ring circuses, his news and commercials, his Master Program), addictedly, on a monitor YOU paid for. (More effective *and* cost-effective.)

And the year itself, diggit: Reagan *had* to be Prez; the Olympics *had* to be staged in L.A. (Vegas wasn't ready yet). There was no irony left in the world.

A year later, when Terry Gilliam's *Brazil* came out, a reviewer or two copped to its taking place, perhaps, in not so much the future as an alternate present, but nobody picked up on it as a film in fact about the *past*—1965, say—a time when Control was still analog, and *occasionally* (in both theory and practice) fallible. A nostalgic little period piece.

AS I LAY DEAD (CHAPTER FROM A NOVEL THE CENTURY WOULD NOT LET ME FINISH)

It's 2035. I've been dead 30 years. Welcome to my treasure trove. My hand-chiseled mausoleum. You and eight or nine others have stumbled in here: *lots* of goodies, take 'em and enjoy! And take your merry time, they ain't going anywhere. Where the hell were you when I was alive?

Ah! the thudding frustration of "slipping through the cracks"—"dying invisible"—or even worse: being branded a "cult writer" (whatever *that* is. Sounds like caves and dungeons. Moonlight); the bitter exhaustion of having to cheerlead my own act, my so-called career (why do we strive? why do we strive?)—fuck *me*. Luck was never mine. Whatever could go wrong, did. Now that it's over, what's the diff? What ever was the diff?

But anyway, come in, take your shoes off, probe and grope me. While I was alive I didn't care much for the notion of scoring—being "discovered"—after I died. It means nothing to me now. "Me" doesn't exist, not anymore, "I" don't either, and "we" never did.

Don't wanna sound like a frigging solipsist (*I die . . . it's over . . . I take it all with me*), it has nothing to do with such piffle. Obviously life goes on—the last reader isn't dead yet— so here's how we maybe should play it: I was generous then (i.e., now: *my* now), always gave the whole wad away, squandered my fluids on writerly whims with but the most esoteric of payoffs, spent 5–6–7 years on books that didn't get me laid, didn't earn me a can of clams, and the bounty of that generosity lingers on. If I can have a corpse, if I can *be* a corpse, so can my work . . . consider it dead. Bountifully. Does death fascinate you?

(While we're on the subject, I sort of doubt my corpse wishes were heeded: to be left naked in the street for the flies to feed on. Please be sure my grave is kept clean.)

Anyway, here 'tis: a gen'rous helping of smut, rant, provocative grocery lists, reviews of wrestling and lubricated condoms, bon mots, lively filler, evidence galore of the author's having ripped the eyes off his face, ripped the skin from his bones and poked it with an icepick, hammered the bones with a claw hammer, lopped them with poultry shears . . . a carload of fine "stuff" from a deadman who knew how!

Hey, I *was* a contender—almost—in the final uneasy days of writing as we the still-living know, er, knew it. Or am I lucky I ever got published at all?

None of which exactly *matters*, y'understand, but it can still be a pisser, still living, to live with it. The taint of "failure." Non-recognition. Something almost like "shame." A cheesy burden on waking consciousness. (Fuck me fatuous.)

And why *do* we strive? Why in the face of setbacks and etc. there aren't sticks (bats) (clubs) enough to shake at, do we persist in *believing* it matters? Damned if *I* know. (Don't give me any hogwash 'bout the "indomitability of the human spirit.")

Listen, I grew up at a time when TV was new . . . none in my home till I was five years old. Imagine such a world (a world also without rock-n-roll). Now you're probably six steps beyond laser discs—I'm talking *your* now. Do "novels" exist anymore? Books as such (without compulsory audio/video/smellorama)? Is "text" just something you at your *option* download off a CD-ROM, database X or Website City, or whatever's replaced them? (Do eyes exist anymore? Do teeth?) This is *not* a science-fiction novel. Or maybe it is. I don't care if you don't.

In any event, behold the document: a "kitchen sink" (as we might once have called it) of life-wish and death-wish and grandiloquent nihility . . . a swag chest knee-deep in glowing all-for-naught . . . a rich accumulation of aromatic dust.

Early in the final decade of the last century, I got interviewed for a French documentary about a 1960s band called the Doors. Their singer was hot shit for a while. "How," I was asked, "would you describe the sexuality they projected?"

Well, I told the guy, making it up as I went along, it wasn't basic rock whiteboy sex of either the '50s or '60s, it wasn't black, y'know, R&B sex, the blues, and it wasn't British-style androgyny or anything especially kinky or even all that topically macho. It wasn't specifically *any* of that so much as— well—it seemed from *this* end, seeing them in this crummy little club every night, like nothing less than a musical evocation of MY OWN dick.

May this heap-o-pulp likewise serve as the ur-expression of YOUR vanity. A foretaste of your own aftertaste, of your own extinction. Don't be shy: use me. I don't mind at all being useful. Let my legacy be your legacy. Fuck legacy. Fuck fuck—I'm a duck.

CONSPIRACIES (1)

Personally, I don't think the CIA killed JFK, and the first click in my head after something reminds me of his snuffout is its position, of all things, in sequence with the rebirth of rock and roll. The snuff occurred in November '63, late, and by the dawning of '64 rock was back again, full force, after being dead in the water since 1958. Really, trust me on this, that *was* the sequence, one two, bing *bing*, in the consciousness/mindset of callow American whiteys my age (18–19)—I was THERE, believe it.

Anyway, back again: doing its trademark mind-body-heart-soul redemption number: the second flowering of rock-roll as such, as an officially so-named whatsit, or if we're talkin' *real* history (or izzit prehistory?), counting the '20s—Delta blues—as the first, and postwar Chicago as the second, early '50s R&B as third, maybe throw in '40s jump blues too, we're looking at possibly the fifth or sixth time it happened (no sweat, tho—it worked): but in any case also its LAST flowering (punk as long as it *was* punk was *something else*).

But flower and flame it did, and no matter how you slice or critique it, by '65-'66 it was like this torch held high in the World—as bright as your proverbial 10 thousand suns—which in congress with certain other factors more or less *formed* the mid to late 1960s—where, regardless of what Clinton and his ilk would prefer you to believe, something, as they say, OCCURRED.

The frigging SIXTIES!—the buzzword, the stereotype, the noumena & phenomena!—plenty of bullshit, too, of course (too kneejerk an Us-versus-Them, too fat and specific a brand new style sheet)—but what did happen was elemental and massive, involving tens of millions of people, a third (easy), maybe even half, of the youth of America, in a just-say-no to toomany things to grocerylist here, and a hogwild hell-yes to even more.

If you wanted to, heck, you could try and isolate a few of the chickens and eggs, some primary causal "culprits." Drugs (natch). Consciousness as a tangible whoozit (and nascent Force). Probably some residual sadness (cynicism) over Kennedy. The ur-loathsomeness of tootoomuch mainstreamamerican life (revealed!) (along with the means, and the warrant, to burn every BRIDGE to it). The hoodoo of the too-long "forbidden," its allure magnified by context to the breaking point: forbidden no more. The demotion of God (from boss to player) in the court of the cosmic and eternal. A provisional end to manymost variants of Judaeo-Christian guilt. Vietnam, the last war with a draft (fear of death at its most functional), gave the whole show mega-sufficient urgency and gravity, but England and Canada didn't have 'Nam, and it happened *there* just as elementally, and maybe even as massively.

And one of the most telling, and most underrecognized, aspects of the whole business is kids, the cognoscenti, having better, livelier things t' do, DIDN'T WATCH TELEVISION.

What they did was hang out with friends, play records, smoke reefer and take pills, stay up all night, carry on, meet and greet the world, and if all else failed they *might* have turned a TV on with the sound off, smoked more reefer and GOOFED ON IT. (These wags nowadays who wanna claim TV helped *radicalize* people in the '60s—news pics of action in the War, for inst—are only looking at a sampling of Old Squares too numb and dumb to have "known" such stuff without the see-Spot-run—not the already converted.)

Oh, and it didn't end suddenly somewhere towards the end of the decade—"decades" have nothing to do with anything, and certainly nothing to do with *this*—but in increments, and by sections. The rock side of things—the torch held high—was hanging much less high by the three-quarter point of '67. Corporatization was rapid-fire and *crass*. "They can't bust our music," read a Columbia Records promo for several of the bands in their "stable," including the hapless Moby Grape (in whose behalf they pulled the inane grandstand play of simultaneously releasing *five singles*, thus doom-ing the truly terrific LP from which they were culled). Too many labels across the board signed (and would never stop signing) too many bands. MGM tried to pull off an "instant scene," the Bosstown Sound—Boston, y'dig?—featuring such happy hokum as Ultimate Spinach. "Alternative culture" came to mean nothing more, nothing less, than alternative product (in the same old, if resized and repainted, market-place).

Even before the '68 Democratic Convention, before even Martin Luther King and Bobby Kennedy got shot, the politi-cal wing—the "Movement," the "Revolution" (ha ha ha), and more concrete (and practical) manifestations like the Panthers—was already gimpy and staggering under the weight of reactive brutality and internal frustration, coupled with diminished ideology. "Purity" is never an easy stance to main-tain.

When at last it finally did end, it was clear it was *over*. Thuddingly. By the spring-summer of '69 (*Easy Rider*, say, then the fucking Moonwalk), everything in counter-land was down the tubes, the toilet, sixty feet under, and with it the last vestige of interest ('cept to necrophiles, archivists and profi-teers) this century. Events after that, from within and with-out, were just nails in coffins, coffins, too many coffins to count. And Manson had nothing to do with it.

Anyway, I *don't* think the CIA killed JFK (with a chess-playing org so concerned with Control, it's hard to believe you would take the KING, and I don't mean Camelot, off the chessboard—especially one whose politics were prob'ly more their own than their founder Truman's, for inst—and expect to retain the social order . . . like he was one of our more RIGHTWING postwar presidents, f'r godsakes, and one so natural to the PR of it all—the source of Reagan!—he had the masses considering him "liberal," a populist, how absurd . . . as to a "splinter group," some buncha renegades, acting independently—against the dominant Agency grain—you've gotta imagine there would've been repercussions, retribution and whatnot, heads would have rolled or at least bounced, conspicuously . . . and mustn't Kennedy have had his PARTISANS inside the Agency? wouldn't there have been some ripples of reaction from *them*? . . . anti-Castro Cubans as perps?—while meanwhile, way after the Bay of Pigs, which the Agency botched, not him, he'd never lost his enthusiasm for KILLING CASTRO—checking the agency's progress towards which was a *daily task* assigned to brother Bobby— I'm not sure why we're s'posed to believe the Cuban faction wasn't a party to, or at least privy to, *that* number . . . as to the need to even shoot the prez, make a martyr out of him for whatever the hell he was or wasn't, there had to 've been e-z ways to neutralize and subdue him—White House fuck tapes? photos of him "doing" Marilyn?—if in fact there was much of anything to subdue . . . heck, if the Agency, if *some* agency, had a hand in undoing Nixon w/out murdering *his* weird ass, why the need for bullets with Kennedy? . . . not to mention he was a literal IVY LEAGUER like manymost of them, an elite goddam player from the getgo, unlike Ike/Dick/Harry/et cetera . . . whereas the prospect of, say, the Mafia—some mob guy whose girlfriend Johnny mighta diddled—committing the deed, eh, now *that* seems eminently credible), yet they certainly didn't waste any time TAKING CREDIT for the deed (so future idiots like Carter and Clinton would be certain they'd done it and never risk "stepping out of line" during their own presidencies), doctoring and creating evidence to the point where relatively little of it, especially the sort of "new evidence" still surfacing at this late remove from the event, is to be trusted; nor do I believe in Conspiracy Theory in general.

Very few designated conspiracies, in fact, would seem to be the outcome of collaborative intrigues, of confederates sitting down at a table, planning you do this, *you* do that, and together we'll fuck with *history*, by gum—they're usually just the inevitable consequence of manypeople—way beyond those at any and all conceivable tables—being simply on the SAME TEAM. Like Foucault, I don't think you need sinister coalitions willfully scheming *anything*—whole entire SHIT-LOADS of folks who'll never meet are already on the same team, and the way teams do their thing hasn't changed much since the dawn of civilization. Did Reagan have to "ask" Hollywood to make the cultural cornerstones of his presidency (*the* enlistment films of the post-braindead multi-decade), *Rambo* and *Top Gun*—or even, for that matter, the soft-sell slop of *Stripes*? Was it really *necessary* to bean-count heads in "both" parties to guess the upshot of Clinton's "impeachment"? Did Bonnie Raitt need to be "cajoled" into vacating the bench of that other team, the long-in-a-slump Peace Team, to lend her careerist "support" to the we-love-our-boys-in-the-fucking-Gulf fandango? (Or might it be, apropos of how a fellow sing-songer had put it, that she jus' wanted to be on the side that appeared, for the moment, t' be winning?)

There are, however, some historical scenarios that look too, too scripted, where unscripted is *extremely* implausible—as if, well, some well-oiled think-tank or somesuch MUST HAVE conceived, coddled, brought them to fruition. "Been responsible" in an originative sense. In this category I put MTV.

Fact: the '60s, whatever did or did not (in reality) go down, scared the shit out of lotsa people in lotsa pockets of power and privilege, your so-called "entrenched" interests, including the grimgrey forces of Death-over-Life per se (you know *them*). Fear. Trembling. A taste of vulnerability (for the previously invulnerable). Were instilled.

Is it plausible that such slaphappy fuckers, their "world" thus threatened, would hesitate a *second*, once the threat had passed, in tossing 'round the bigbucks, funding to the TEETH any and all nefarious efforts to ensure that nothing similar would ever go down again?—or at the very least, failing to achieve such omnipotence, and since accidents do happen, to see to it that some failsafes be in place to limit the damage?—is it plausible they'd pass THAT up?

Enter: one or more mercenary "study groups," gaggles of amoral brainstormers—pay 'em, they'll without compunction piss on any world including their own. If happyfolks at the Rand Corporation (as we later were told) dropped acid and sat around discussing ways of winning nuclear war—fun & games w/ the Apocalypse—imagine what a hoot some favored colleagues had in running down the psychedelic '60s.

And a prime ensuing "project," it sez here, was to make sure American youth got their full dose of TV like ev'ryone else (come rain or shine).

Becuz here were these pricks who (upon reflection, and after research) DID notice how many kids had passed on "the tube" from such a date to such a date. And *why* didn't they watch? For starters, the obvious: the sorry dearth of televised rock on a regular basis. There was all the Dick Clark shit, sure—ersatz till you upchuck—and occasional name guests on *Ed Sullivan* or *The Smothers Brothers*, but nothing to set your watch by. As a youth sop, *Mod Squad* fooled no one with two-tenths of a brain (and it didn't have cameos by actual bands). (Only 8-year-olds watched *The Monkees*.)

Needed: a viable means of both showcasing and neutralizing (compromising) a steady stream of frontline rock on the home screen.

So however these things work . . . seeds planted . . . circumstances tweaked . . . record companies goosed (dig this new marketing tool) . . . a slow, steady groundswell of greed fomented . . . advertisers felt up and out (let 'em think it's *their* idea) . . . greasing the wheels (c'mon, *somebody* greased 'em—y'don't buy the MTV "instant success story," do ya?) . . . say, isn't that former Monkee Michael Nesmith over there? . . . until finally, early '80s, here 'tis: an actual rock-roll *channel*. Network. Crowd control module. Whatever.

By which time, in the wake of punk having bit the dust, then circled back itself t' join the marketplace, rock on its own was already not about redemption (or liberation) (or empowerment) or anything close, and couldn't wait to comply: the wundaful world-o-videos. (Monkee-ization of the whole shebang.) When the frigging MINUTEMEN did a vid, you knew it was *completely* over. The commercial, the come-on, *was* the product, the thingie, the "art form." Where once there had at least been a semblance of polarity, of a dialectic (the Big Score vs. unbridled Whoopee Per Se), now you had none. Rock and the marketplace were *indivisibly* one, no separation, not even an argument, just like TV and the 'place: an early warning that dialectical materialism (as we knew it on earth) would soon give way to unrepentant MATERIALISM. For the rest of our lifetimes, anyway.

FINE TIME TO BE BORN

Couldn't be finer.

May 11, 1945. Dizzy Gillespie's "Salt Peanuts" is recorded in New York. Though not the original version, this is the ONE, with players including not only Charlie Parker but Sid Catlett, arguably the greatest drummer jazz has produced (more sizzling *in context*, it could be shown, than Elvin Jones at his Coltrane-era best), and it's probably produced more great-great A–1 drummers than A–1 alto sax players. Parker, 24, the highwater mark for alto, jazz's most mind-blowing soloist (any instrument), and prob'ly the greatest musician (period) ever to record a note, would be dead in less than 10 years. Gillespie, a more cautious breed of hellion, would live to perform "Salt Peanuts" at the White House, with guest vocal by peanut farmer Jimmy Carter: great moments in kitsch.

I'm one day old.

If I'd been born just two days earlier, my parents would later claim, they'd've named me Victor—for V-E Day—how lucky can ya get?

And luckier still for THIS, and its ilk, to have been the music stirring and shaking the air, if not down the block then close enough, in the very town where I entered this life, though it would be 17 years (during one of rock's major *down times*) before I would fortuitously get t' hear it: frenzied, frenetic, frantic—stop, start, fly, floop, over and out—go 'head, call it *nutty*. But not nutty like Spike Jones, or *Hellzapoppin* or a Bugs Bunny cartoon: nutty like a miracle in the wilderness.

NUTTY, RECENT, WHITE

Twenty anagrams for "Twentieth Century":

THERE WENT UN-CITY T. (Trumancapoteville: that-away); HENCE U RENT TWITTY (y'need Conway for a party, so you pay for him); WHUT TEN-C ETERNITY? (*what* endless import, 10 centuries?—"millennia" debunked); IRENE NETTY "T.W." CHUT (1914–76, proponent of "tough weakness" therapy for substance abuse); TENT-CUT THY WIENER (so sayeth Leviticus, one O.T. scholar insists); W.C.T.E.: 'NUTHER ENTITY? (is the Women's Christian Temperance Enfederation *really* diff'rent from their Union?);

HY TRICE WENT T' *UTNE* (Hyman Trice, co-founder of the
Utne Reader, went there straight from *McCall's*); WET TEN-
INCH RYE TUT (medium-size Egyptian novelty bread, after
the rain); TENTH WETT-URINE CY. (nine, make that *ten*
cyclopses, consecutive, whose pee ain't dryy); CHEWY TINT-
NET—TRUE (*no lie* about edible dyed women's hose); TUN-
NEY ET IT W/ "H" CERT (Gene followed lobster with a
heroin-flavor breath mint); HEY, T.R. WENT T' TUNECI (no
shit: Teddy Roosevelt attended classes at the Technical Univ.
of Northeast Connecticut, Illimantic); NEUTER THE
WITTY N.C. (Noël Coward should be *desexed*, humorless
critics contend); TEEN WINE TRUTH: C.Y.T. (choose your
toxin, kids); TWIN TRUENCY TEETH (geez: she cut school
twice t' visit the dentist!); RECENT N.U. WYETH TIT
(*exceptional* breast painting by Andy Wyeth's unheralded
cousin, Napoleon Ulysses Wyeth); *WUTHERIN' TENCTETY*
(Emily Brontë's turgid, yet still unpublished, sequel to
Wuthering Heights); T. IN THE EYE, 'TWURN'T "C" ('twas
only English Breakfast, *not* cancer, thank fuck); *TUNE THE Y.
WIRE* (CTNT) (made-for-Canadian-cable film o' the year for
'93); YET THE WINTER CUNT . . .

RAUNCH CORRELATION

Obviously, centuries don't exist. Not like days, nights, seasons, or years do.

Ten fingers (Caesar had them, as do we), hence the deci-
mal system.

In long retrospect or short, sequences, chronologies, linkages could doubtless be otherwise. All ascription of the squawk of moment, of its raunch correlation with neighboring moments (and the longer haul), more than, oh, two years after the fact is purely revisionist.

It so happens the 20th ends *now*. If it ended in 1956 or '57, unencumbered by the anathema such truck would entail today, we could conceivably be discussing, even in this exalted alt-weekly, gross inanities like GREAT CHICKS (HOT BROADS) (BOSS BABES) OF THE CENTURY (Josephine Baker . . . Harlow . . . Lana . . . Ava . . . *your ballot* on page 52!); might even be proposing, in the afterglow of her lurid bump through *The Girl Can't Help It* (co-starring Little Richard), Jayne Mansfield as THE manwoman of the whole cha-cha-cha.

Is there not something grossly revisionist, in a very real sense, that only a current menu of options—contexts—perspectives is "legitimately" considered?

THE TOWEL

Complicity.

We all comply at times in our own undoing.

Lots-o-persons in most lines of etc. have thrown in the towel, but for *writers* to have done it as early as they did was a particularly bad omen, a foretoken of just how quickly and nastily *all* the dominoes would fall.

Sheesh . . . it's downright *tragic*.

Writepersons, who at least in theory should know better, and who dealing in words and ideas and such crap—keepers as they are of the oldest flame going: the flame of MEAN-ING—bear a certain, uh, responsibility for and to the welfare of all livingthings, well they shoulda knowed right off the bat what it *meant*.

Publishers of newspapers & mags, to save money, make things "go faster," started firing typesetters, and the writers for these rags became typesetters, what they turned in was already *set*, but no savings or perks of any sort were passed on to them. Editors, editing on these little screens, fucked up more than before, stupider typos, more ridiculous line breaks, as copy routinely got mangled. The only side of writing that one could argue had been improved was the clerical side (hey, y'mean I don't gotta retype? it'll check my spelling?—gosh), never the creative side.

Nor the economic side. Where once all anyone needed t' write was a pencil, suddenly you had to INVEST IN all this ugly machinery, the equivalent of a washer-dryer-aircondi-tioner. And that clickety-clack typer that'd served your techno needs—manual; electric; even a Selectric—well it won't write to disc or double as a printer, so chuck it: a useless antique.

In '91, after being told by every paper I worked for that if I didn't submit copy on disc I would hafta come in and retype it into their computer anyway, I succumbed to the coercion and bought my first computer. Not wanting to be distracted by superfluous opticals—I'm a writer, 's not a hobby, don't insult me with *toys*—I got a monochrome monitor. My first impression was of having to drive to work—to work at home. A bleary-eyed commuter. It made the process of writing so unpleasant that the genesis of paragraphs, pages, pieces ultimately took me *longer*.

Today, with e-mail and the Internet and truckloads of unwanted "applications" and vid-games and Zip drives and scanners and all the standard compulsory whatnot—shit I don't want, and don't want to *need*—it feels like I've bought this car that was out of my range, and I also had to shell out for 7000 teddy bears and a million pairs of purple socks and a 300-year subscription to *Field and Stream*. Ninety-nine percent superfluity. (Every second I'm sitting at the fucker, I feel like I've been HAD.)

"Personal" computers: nobody needs th'm. It isn't *about* need! Well, animators for the graphics on *Monday Night Football* need th'm, but FUCK the animation on *Monday Night Football*. The world would go on fine without it.

Coercion. Fooling ostensibly all of the people closer, ever closer, to all of the time. Soon we'll be expected to pay our goddam bills online, and if y'ain't on it yourself you'll have to subscribe to a service that does it for you. How long before we gotta pay to breathe? Don't know *your* take on this madness, but it's the bitter END of mammal life as I used to know it.

The stations of my loathing . . .

I basically haven't watched TV news since 1980, or about the time Jimmy Carter reinvented the Cold War, table-setting the Reagan years. The fraudulence of this prick's daily TV PER-

FORMANCE, the sick macho gesture of an Annapolis wuss who'd used coverage of Three Mile Island (him in a spacesuit) to prime the pump—this to me was what the Cuban Missile Crisis had been to others . . . *never again*. My decision wasn't driven by escapism—an attempt to avoid knowing "what was going on." I simply no longer wanted any part of Master Control's by-the-numbers show & tell—the sights, the sounds, the easy trifling with every sinew of our being.

Likewise, with computers, it is not bad enough that they exist and are heinous and more or less mandatory. Knowing that is merely knowing that, but to SEE its ubiquitous face is to BE THERE yourself, witness to the SAME pinks, luminous greys, cerulean blues, all the dings and dongs from cyber hell, which constitute the universal workspace of the damned, lockstepping to the horror, the horror.

A future-vision straight out of Disney, or to be precise, *Disneyland* the original weekly series. Several times each, they'd served up pap from Fantasyland, Frontierland, and Adventureland before finally, in '54 or '55, they aired the first Tomorrowland segment—some unremarkable animations of space flight shown-and-told by Werner von Braun. With much cash, effort, and national sacrifice, said the denazified Nazi of the hour, we might make it to the moon by the year 2000 . . . ooh, wouldn't *das* be *wunderbar*.

Well, they never did get us there, the bastards, but they also never lost the pre-rock fiftiesness of the dream, which they assault us with today WITHOUT MERCY: Eisenhowerland!: whitebread über alles!: thesauruses w/out the word "shit"!: mall-world before malls! A perfect formica simulation—do they even *make* that stuff anymore?—that's what I see on MY so-called desktop (don't know 'bout yours). On which must be endured an endless procession of ads for shit I don't want/need/wanna know about. Every screaming *icon* is a product i.d. How long before you click on "save" and there's an ad for some fucking bank?

All this "virtual" bullticky—addresses that aren't addresses, access that isn't access, e-mail "relationships"—is bogofication more ludicrous (and hideous) than made-for-TV movies of the '70s and '80s. "User friendly," what a laugh—as bogus as "have a nice day"—while an elite core of PLUMBERS are the only ones who even *sometimes* know the bowels of the operation, what's indeed *going on*. This isn't relative unreality, but the *absolute* unreality of it all—as sham as a speech by Pat Robertson. Or is an absolute *anything* no longer feasible?

Why don't people read books anymore? Because after a day at the office in front of a freakin' screen, they're TOO BLIND to read a book. Fewer books being read, and fewer being bought, "literature" is no longer a relevant category at a major U.S. publishing house—true!—you could call 'em up and ask. Coffee table garbage, self-help, textbooks, designated bestsellers, and of course computer books—such is our current literary lot. And I'm not talking "good writing" vs. "bad writing," I'm talking language as a solemn goddam cross to bear—writing as a taking of risks as large as life (when it was still large) itself.

There is more need right now to unplug from the prevailing "real world" scam than there was in the '60s. Are you man/woman enough?

1969

The year instant replay became standard for major league baseball, not merely for homers and crucial fielding plays but practically every pitch ("Curve ball, low and away, Ralph").

An accursed season not even redeemed by the up-from-the-sewer N.Y. Mets snatching the World Series.

This wurn't no simple, gratuitous *recoverability* number, like reruns of old films or "oldies but goodies," the concept/package introduced on AM radio around 1960, but something (in the scheme of things) genuinely pernicious: the undermining of spectator consciousness.

An end to unidirectionality . . . to events in time *heading somewhere* . . . to time/expired actually meaning something.

PLUS: the root beginnings of nonstop cross-cut sports editing (with hyperactive fans and players' wives and the crippled kid who's got a month to live and all o' *that*), employing "cinematic" means to manipulate the perception of real-time events *in* real time, thus rendering *space* permanently *un*real (first done "experimentally," and with major malice, in the live broadcast of the JFK funeral some five-plus years before), a follow-the-dots aimed at more than a quaint li'l studio audience: the stay-at-home sporting masses, bub!

Our first taste of such as STANDARD MALICIOUS BROADCAST PROCEDURE.

1920

A *very* early warning.

In his first novel, the *Less Than Zero* of its time, F. Scott Fitzgerald plays the hole card of socialism, only his socialism is quitelike fascism, and not just the way it might *transmute* into something like fascism, y'know down the road, like when Stalin would go and do all these purges (and pogroms) in an excess of institutional whatever, but fascism *already*, originally, pretty much by definition.

In short order, *This Side of Paradise* would sell 2 million copies, a prototype of the literary killing for ages-to-come of young American doodooheads, and make its author (the emperor's new clothes of mock-modernist trend-think; jock-sniffer to the Rich decades before Capote, Tom Wolfe, or P.J. O'Rourke; debaser of the concept of "jazz" before it was even a *third* of a concept; grandfather, godfather—or simply harbinger?—of the Yuppie) the toast of who fucking gives a shit.

Imagine the play he'd've got on *Entertainment Tonight* or PBS. 'S a good thing, in those days, only the *literate* were subject to such crap.

CONSPIRACIES (2)

Why do you think Nixon abolished the draft? Not from compassion, that's for sure. No draft = no draft resistance. Or much resistance, or protest—as opposed to mere *objection*—to anything, really. Why do you think there's no perceptible leftist presence, nor even much of a *politics*, among the formerly draftable (18 and up) anymore?

AIDS. Not too many're claiming anymore it was custom-designed—scientists (outside of fiction) just ain't that ingenious—or even, especially, that somebody in fact *invented* it. It would still seem, howev, that at some point, by hook or by crook—"accident"? "discovery"? "engineering"?—whoever *they* were had something on their hands, this virus, this bug—what t' do with it? First off, let's see what it can *do*—who'll we test it on?

And why does it seem likely it *was* tested? 'Cuz epidemiologically, ha, there apparently is NO WAY (contrary to the usual "explanation") for AIDS to have gone from being a heterosexually based epidemic (in Africa) to a homosexual one (in the U.S., "via Haiti"—or so the story went) *as rapidly as it did*. It isn't even a longshot—it's off the actuarial page. Demographic breakdowns on early HIV distribution—the earliest hints of outbreak—point, out of all proportion, to recipients of an experimental hepatitis B vaccine tested exclusively on gay U.S. men, and of a tainted batch of smallpox vaccine administered by health workers in Africa. Tested, inotherwords, on a pair of population groups—blacks and gays—deemed *expendable*.

From genocide to mass-manipulating the living. Once the virus was out there, the policy among the elite that *knew* (however much or little) was to let it flourish, reveal nothing that might prove helpful in saving a life or umpteen thousand. If junkies and hookers were soon getting sick, fine, that's cool—who needs either o' *them*, either? By which point new malevolents were "joining" the plot, hopping the bandwagon, to make damnsure there would be no needle exchanges, no free condoms, no encouraging people to just beat off already, no advice to anyone except just say no, and by all means keep away from queers—demonized this time around as the source of pestilence. (And what, pray tell, *is* the Ameri-Christian beef with homosexuality? That it is, bottom line, from their tightassed perspective, prima facie *sexual*—the very word conjures up images of sex *acts*—sperm flying all over the place—while the fact of Donnie Osmond, say, as a professed heterosexual evokes *nothing*.) When the bandwag reached its broadest mass-media phase, the evil got more omni-directed, and the goal, clearly, became one of trying to SCARE THE SEX OUT OF EVERYONE. Hedonism = freedom . . . fuh . . . it'd gone on long enough. One custom-designed consequence: an upswing in hetero monogamy—gee, how sweet— to nudge the birth rate up another notch.

Disposable diapers. As the '60s were waning, the American birth rate was at a postwar low. This at a moment when young'uns were fucking like krazy—and abortion was still, in most places, illegal—so how to 'splain it? More important for corporate America, how to overcome it?—to reattach babies to the sex urge?—get some economic mileage out of orgaz and ejaculation? Whaddaya think the REAL objection to abortion is in high U.S. places? Squeezing votes from the most easily led of constituencies is small potatoes—there's always other ways, too many ways, to pull those people's chains. Nah, chalk it up to corporate greed. Corporations always want MORE mouths to feed, and bodies to dress, and suburban commuters to sell cars and gas and garage door openers to, and more occasions to market topical relief to more sufferers from a life more inhospitable every day. If it ain't more, it's as bad as less. Plus: more unwanted (and unterminated) pregnancies means more neurosis in the world, which means more consumers consuming neurotically, thus micro-manageably, on corporate dotted lines.

For the record: starting during Reagan's first term, and no diff due to a Democrat taking office, the U.S. has done its utmost to dismantle every third-world birth control program it helped initiate in the first place. Keep 'em hungry, keep 'em needy, sell 'em more and bigger Bruce Willis movies—keep those debtor nations under our boot! The Population Explosion, that late-'50s cause célèbre—when there were only *two* billion people in the world—what ever happened to THAT? (And don't tell me Ben & Jerry name flavors for it.)

So anyway . . . births . . . '60s . . . down . . . how come? And somewhere on the massive list of "reasons" some research outfit ultimately compiled—way, way after the important stuff you can't do much about, in some cases 'cause *you* caused it, oh, like the unlivability of life (y'know at this stage of decay on the planet); the basic expansion of people's moral conscience over their parents' (the karma stops here); the magnanimous avoidance of the sheer ego-puke of "*my* son, *my* daughter . . . *mein* kampf"; the polygamization of p.o.v. (even if you're only *sequentially* lining up alternate partners, off-spring complicate breakup and mobility); the cost of baby food, baby shoes, the cost of . . . college (none o' *that* gettin' cheaper); a simple, basic refusal to get sucked in, go with the program (better to stick your nose in a garbage disposal)—down near the bottom had to be diapers: *who wantsa deal with 'em?* To dissuade that marginal minipercent to whom such b.s. might somehow be a deciding factor, voilà:

Disposable diapers (but won't they pollute the earth?)—who could ask for anything more?

Since then we've had ovarian vogue . . . the culture of babying . . . 10 billion baby films . . . a population increase of 70 million (U.S. alone). Dominoes, anyone?

RED HERRING OF THE CENTURY

Child abuse. Child abuse?

All parenting *is* abuse. (Sure as meat is murder, property is theft.)

Physical abuse bothers you? Well, what about spiritual abuse?

My idea of a major felony: inflicting on a child, age 0–12, the concept of heaven and hell. Especially hell.

"Teaching" a kid hell oughta be worth a mandatory minimum of 20, no, 30 years. On a fuckin' chain gang. No lunch breaks. (Don't let *nobody* say I'm soft on crime.)

In its sorry, sordid end run, has "religious freedom" as practiced in this country ever done much more than buck up the right, the compulsion!, of various afflicted grownups to perpetuate the germplasm of whatever strain of fire-and-brimstone they themselves were once branded with, i.e., to inflict their ongoing dogma on innocent, unmolded lumps of dough? And what of the rights of goddam dough? Where are all our "victim's rights" advocates on this one?!

If Satanism, whatever the bloody hell, in theory or practice, that even is (though a 'ligion, like all others, f'r sure), can be systematically denied Constitutional protection, then *phuck* its hand-in-glove "opposite" number.

(Crowd control in the ozone, crowd control from hell.)

Likewise:

The "threat" of pornography to today's unwashed youth (on or off the Internet).

Dunno about you, but I wouldn'ta made it to 13 without pics in smutmags to cue me to what the whole wide world of carnal oo-poo-pa-doo was ABOUT.

The aforementioned Jayne! Mansfield!—hoo wee!—tits out to HERE—first nipples I saw on anyone 'sides my mother: oh nurture! Just a peek, mind you—mags back then didn't really show *that* much—but otherwise there'd've been no peek, nothin'.

1956: forty-three years ago. We're supposed to believe preadolescents need this shit less TODAY? (Pshaw.)

Denying them porn would be abusive.

MODS

Some cheezier modifications of the record:

Cus D'Amato as a "fine boxing mind"—as opposed to just the formulator of an ultra-safe "Floyd Patterson strategy." Floyd lacked ferocity ("killer instinct"), grit, guts, nerve, much of a punch, even so-so footwork, and a chin—a lot to cover for. All he was was fast. So Cus matched him against nonentities—Roy Harris, Pete Rademacher—and even these clowns embarrassed Floyd, knocking him down in early rounds, though through the accumulation of punches he ultimately triumphed—big deal—the most unloved heavyweight champion since Jack Sharkey.

Only because of his short-lived connection to Mike Tyson, whose stock-in-trade, when he was still on, was ferocity unleashed, plus enough power in either hand to take out a mule, things beyond being taught, was Cus, in his lifetime, ever regarded as anything but a marginal schmuck.

The title of an article in *Sport* magazine around '58 or '59, before Floyd got KO'ed by Ingemar Johansson, whom Cus regarded lightly (he was European, see) or he wouldn't've allowed the fight, said it all: *The Terrible World of Cautious Cus.*

And try this on for size:

The Beatles will not fare well in the new century, if only 'cause the full gamut of their once-accessible sonic past no longer exists. 'Cept on warped, scratched vinyl, and when they stop making record needles, that's that. By going beyond normal remastering to REMIX certain "classic" Beatle cuts for CD reissue, Paul McCartney has canceled any ongoing role for *them*—except as an adjunct, largely mythical, to his own vanity. Devastated in the process is music (yes: music; not recollected youth! not sociology!) an even billion people have got stored in their heads, their hearts, their bones—and can imagine verywell, having memorized every nuance—but will never HEAR, as pulsating masses of air, again. (Unless they're enterprising rich fucks who can score lingering undebased analog sources and do what they fucking want, formatwise, with the sonic genepool. Otherwise, from here on out, there *is* no sonic genepool.)

Which is kinda like taking some print classic like *Huckleberry Finn*, something read and reread for the last 100 years if for no other reason than it's always been *there*, burning all copies, then issuing it in BRAILLE ONLY, or on the backs of oatmeal boxes (in Greek).

For ex.: "Penny Lane," a full half, along with "Strawberry Fields," of the second greatest two-sided hit of all time (after "Hound Dog"/"Don't Be Cruel"), was originally a very decent treble-heavy song, but in remix Paulie brought his bass way up, and the drums feel different too, and it all sounds *between two places* (almost like the Drifters' "There Goes My Baby," an early, not totally successful, rock experiment with strings), which it didn't before, it felt indivisible—it's not the same song, not even close. And it's more offensive when we get to a Lennon song, "Baby You're a Rich Man," on which John played this squeaky, spooky, very interesting keyboard thing (a clavioline?)—it was WHAT made the recording so engaging—that's now mixed down, and Paul's bass is up again—it sounds like crap. (Plus John is dead, eh?) These two cuts heard in sequence, on the CD version of *Magical Mystery Tour*, are particularly exasperating, they make me *gag*.

What's this cheesepuff solipsist worth, 8 billion dollars? Why can't he leave this shit alone?

BEATS "R" US

Mea culpa, mea culpa. Yes, I have colluded in denigrating, sullying, STINKING UP the Beat archive. Can't you smell it?

The redolence of coffee, of Starbucks, and of coffee tables.

There's probably been more unmitigated bullcrap written about the Beats than any quantitatively similar culture scene, including white probes of black music and all the dumb inquiries-cum-exploitations of the hippie '60s. John Updike scolded the Beats as bratty, self-involved children; that academic slime Norman Podhoretz called them leather-jacketed savages with zipguns: these too-generous, too-virtuous rogue pilgrims whose writings were as perfect an antidote to '50s Drear as rock & roll, as sublimely uplifting, if less *instantaneously* magical (you had to spend time and *read 'em*).

And NOW, folks: the coffee table blasphemy of *The Rolling Stone Book of the Beats* (1999). While not the first c.t. Beat book—Allen Ginsberg did at least three c.t.'s on his own (as opposed to just large format, 9x11, like the posthumous Kerouac whatzis, *Some of the Dharma*)—it's one of the heavier ones with more text than pixtures . . . and I've got the longest thing in it.

An edit-down of a five-year-old article originally called "Another Superficial Piece about 176 Beatnik Books"—they cut me down to 158—but it's anything *but* superficial: a stone-serious take on Beat as writ and published . . . text as direct emanation of self . . . the intersection of kicks and *cellular concern* . . . the poetryprose of let's-get-naked-for-10-minutes-and-maybe-tell-the-truth—if we fail, at least we tried, y'hear? I talk about all 158, and I rave loud and long 'bout Kerouac's *Big Sur* as one of the ur-masterpieces of the English language . . . and Lew Welch as the greatest Romantic y'never heard of . . . and I make sure you know about Philip Whalen and Bob Kaufman and John Wieners . . . and Jack Micheline and Peter Orlovsky and Hettie Jones . . . 'cause if you don't, well, your life is that much poorer. Nothin' on my part to be embarrassed about, I guess, but, but . . . I dunno.

Shoot, there were some very suspect early Beat collections that included people like NORMAN MAILER, someone about as Beat (or Beat-cognizant) as Tony Curtis. Thank heck he's not in this one, but take a look at the sad parade of interlopers, slummers, and party poopers who are: Yoko Ono, Johnny Depp, Lee Ranaldo, Deborah Harry, Graham Nash . . . Graham Nash? My erstwhile pal Patti Smith, as phony as 80 days are long, whom I remember in '71 calling Ginsberg "that Jew queer," contributes the gushing, almost toesucking "Dear

Allen" (p. 274). On p. 307, Don Waller, a slick-haired hepcat wanna-be, the 2nd or 3rd jivest person I've ever met, one of that vast army of jerks who have made the term "cool" useless till the end of time, makes the claim that "Any serious discussion of 'Beat humor' starts with Lord Buckley and Lenny Bruce"—no it doesn't!

Nor were the Beats themselves especially "hipsters"—sure they were, but they were also distinctly (and distinctively) not-that, and some—Ferlinghetti, John Clellon Holmes, Carl Solomon—were not-that, period. Kerouac once presented his take on karmic responsibility as "No rest until every sentient being is redeemed"—show me the hipster in *them* apples, Don.

Listen, *I'm* no Beatnik—born in '45, you can't be one in much more than spirit (unless you're Anne Waldman, who based on her connection to Ginsberg at Naropa, though she isn't even small-b *beat*, often gets tapped the youngest "actual" Beat) (Trixie A. Balm, eat yer heart out)—but at least I've got some *respect*, see, for those that truly be.

Ain't tryin' to rain on anybody's interlope party, but I hold this stuff *sacred*, okay?

And it gives me a creepy feeling to be in a volume so brimming w/ not only coffee grounds but alien SCUZZ.

So why *am* I in the damn thing? Why have I given it my consent? Hey: I even participated in a reading at Borders to hype sales. I give it my consent for the illusion of visibility, the self-deception of a mission of truth, and last but not least, a check for three figures.

WHALE OF A POET

Freud.

As *dandy* a poet as Catullus, Blake, Baudelaire, Rimbaud, Dickinson, Whitman, Pound, Ginsberg, or Ogden Nash.

Now that everything he wrote has been devalued from science to hermeneutics ("interpretation"), while Jung is classed (and revered) as some weird sort of pagan mystic, and frontline beatniks never lost their affection for Reich, let's just keep Siggy around for what he most IS: an ole-fashioned coke & tobacco *motherfucker* whose unabashed MAGNILO-QUENCE puts him up there with Freddie Blassie and Rabelais.

Poetry: the root, if not route, of ALL philosophy (and science!) worthy of the name.

ED WOOD VS. COCTEAU:
WHO WILL WIN?

The notion of Greatness—the judgment, the sentiment, the nervous tic: great albums, great cinematographers, great draft beers—do we really need to waste our time on that worn and weary road? Is it any longer an attribution of anything pertinent—germane—worth a bucket of owl spit?

The rise! the fall! (the bloody persistence) of Charisma. As in *the charismatic Brad Pitt*—a dishrag who "looks like James Dean."

The April '98 *Gentlemen's Quarterly*, a "special collector's issue," pays tribute to the Athlete of the Century, Muhammad Ali. There was a time, back when I was more immersed in boxing, when I'd've called him the Man, the Manwoman, the PERSON of the Century. Of course, no doubt, beyond all hype, he *is* the sportsperson of the 20th, just as he was with 25 years still remaining, and his '74 knockout of Foreman in Zaire stands as one of the two or three most conspicuous public achievements since, well, after my own arbitrary cutoff date, '69-'70.

But achievement, merit—what *is* the cash value (in the William Jamesian sense) of either of THOSE curios at century's end? Possibly they *never* meant a fuck of a lot without the requisite hype, without a coercive lesson plan for dumbass mortals, a hierarchic see-Spot-run of canonical More to our abject Less . . . so good riddance. And in one sense at least, if still below the level of reflexive consciousness, of our common awareness, I think we *are* rid of one twang of the shuck: "high" art vs. "low."

And I don't mean 'cause people in gen'ral seem more, more?, maybe more *attracted* to lowstuff like gothic romance or yuppie sitcoms or whatever, which isn't really even the low I'm getting at (that stuff's just lowest common denom, and what's at issue here is lower than the denom—low as in lowlife: gutter stuff)—I mean that among incrementally more of those who not long ago would've been patrons of high, exclusively, it's no longer as systematically, or as automatically, exclusive (with or without the alibi of "guilty pleasure").

And like I said, not too many of these geeks are actually, wakingly aware of it, but habits of valuation have changed—slightly—there's a certain piecemeal laxing of the rigor—even among those of 'em you can fool all of the time.

DADA come home to roost? Duchamp (et al.) propheteering? Hardly.

Marcel Duchamp, who abandoned "retinal art" not long after painting the arch-retinal *Nude Descending a Staircase*, was one of the supreme foreshadows of the early 20th, even begetting a workable copy—a xerox—a silk screen, anyway—in Andy Warhol, but his wisdom, his shrewdness, his cool-customerhood would have been as zilch without an adventitious mass means of activating some mighty riffs (as infantile as they are intellectual) lurking in *everyone's* art-critical toolbag, of deconstructing sundry impractical (but ingrained) valuational norms, of delivering the package on a bedrock of common utility, of normal situational perception, and that means was/is/has been—to the extent that it has been AT ALL—not the beats, not Pop Art, not the hippies, not punk, not specifically anyway, but rock & fucking roll—the Whole Damn Thing—45 years down its long & winding pike, still rolling (clunkily) on.

The massive means, the massive hap, the massive rub. To even *begin* to collapse, demolish, reduce (or at least fuzz over) crucial distinctions in the public eye between high and low, we've needed more years of rock than it's actually functioned *as* rock (as opposed to as Big Culture, or as Typical Showbiz, or as Monster Trucks Soundtrack): the '50s, '60s, '70s, '80s, *and* '90s . . . longggg after it ceased being useful for much of anything else . . .

If you view them with an open heart and an unjaundiced eye, Jean Cocteau's *Orpheus*, the celebrated "art pic" of 1950, and Edward D. Wood's *Night of the Ghouls*, "celluloid trash" from '59, offer surprisingly, yet undeniably, similar takes on Death and the Other Side, but the bottom line is this: Wood is what Cocteau is trying to be, he's a Cocteau pulling no punches, (put this in his résumé!) COCTEAU WITHOUT RESTRAINT. *Testament of Orpheus*, meanwhile, the Frenchman's pretentious '60 sequel, is the stale sweat of a sweaty poet, while the meagerest works of Wood radiate sheer delight.

(Wood: you might know him from Tim Burton's less than flattering *Ed Wood*, '94, which doesn't *completely* mock the guy's work, heckles it mostly in fun, but stops far short of true admiration. At least, tho, they now got some actual Wood films at the video store, at *more* video stores. For starters, I recommend *Bride of the Monster*.)

No more Art (sent or received) on a pedestal: wouldn't *that* be nice!

BOBO

Carl "Bobo" Olson, born July 11, 1928, Honolulu. "The Hawaiian Swede."

Champion? Also-ran? Both.

Great? Not-great? Not-great.

Overreacher? Underachiever? Overreacher.

Interesting? Interesting enough . . .

In '53, following the retirement of Sugar Ray Robinson, won 15-round decisions over Paddy Young and Randy Turpin to gain recognition as world middleweight champ.

June '55, moving up in weight, challenges Archie Moore for the lightheavyweight title and is knocked out in the 3rd round. In December, Robinson (unretired) KO's Bobo in 2, recapturing the middleweight crown, and in the rematch six months later, in 4.

1960: campaigning as a lightheavy, with pretensions of moving up to heavyweight, he is kayoed in 6 by an up-and-coming Doug Jones, the first serious challenge (two years later) for the young Cassius Clay.

Career continues through '66. Final record: 92–16–2. In the end: broke.

Rumors of bigamy? Of two entire families in different cities? Um . . . uh . . . that's more or less correct.

Did someone say bozo?

STALER BREAD, GRIMMER CIRCUS

> My wife's been sick, the young'uns too,
> And I'm durn near down with the flu,
> The cow's gone dry and them hens won't lay,
> But we're still a-livin', so ever'thing's okay.
>
> —"Everything's Okay," Luke the
> Drifter (Hank Williams)

The commoditization of despair . . . the "populism" of universal slip-slide . . . the no-future of an illusion . . . the mega-marketing of leaner pickings.

In 1980, during the Iran hostage crisis (and the CIA's Afghan incursion), *Slash* editor Claude Bessy, a/k/a Kickboy Face, punk-rock's hottest voice-in-print, announced, without a trace of grief: "We will not live to see the end of this decade"—he figured Carter would be blowing up the planet any day. "I only regret," he added, "that I won't live to see *enough* of the horror." Slightly later, after the threat had subsided (but why forget its sting?), *Slash* reviewer Chris D. hailed some German punk LP as "adequate sonic preparation for the heat-death of the world." Torment, torture, and subjugation *as* the trip . . . dig it.

The X Files: of *course* they lie to us—or is it simply we'll believe anything? Either way, the endless wellspring of a real *kink* of a show . . . both ABOUT the ruse and the ruse ITSELF . . . *Twilight Zone*, or is it *Gilligan's Island?*, as *60 Minutes* . . . escapism and surrender at the same time, in the same breath . . . can't wait for the next episode!

David Cronenberg's *eXistenZ*: the abhorrent *yuck* of what cybershit hath wrought, and of what we've been duped into *demanding* from it . . . done as perhaps the most seamlessly, elegantly crafted LSD movie, ever.

KEROUAC NEVER DROVE, SO HE NEVER DROVE ALONE

You're born alone, you die alone, you pull into a 20th century truckstop alone where every trucker looks like the devil.

Like pictures of the devil. Like they'd kill you worse than cops or buy you a beer, two beers, if they knew what you were thinking. About their looking like the devil or killing you or buying you beers. But there's no beer at this stop, so it's only devil, killing . . .

GOODBYE PORKPIE CRAVAT

There is a box
and in the box is the shit of God
There is a bag
and down at the bottom is a Vicks inhaler
busted open with the cotton removed
long gone and whistling
in the brains and belly of Lester Eugene Bangs

There is a bump
on the head of Lester that (he says)
only Romilar can cure
("Look, it's working already!"
—it's such an *unsightly* bump)
There is an edge
and the edge is Lester's home and hearth
365 endless big ones a year
(spin on that axis so that Lester may spin
with the wind)

There is a smell

worse than Lester but no one has smelt it
There is a "cleaned-up Lester" (alleged)
smelling like roses but the roses are dead
There is an urn
in El Cajon with petals burned and blistered
smelling like John Morthland's Luckies in a tray
(There is a life
and in this life so-and-so is fucked)

PERSON WHO'S DEAD

for Peter Ivers

His life was like a fart.

Y'know:

first part

second part

third part

FOURTH part.

THE OLD FUCKEROO

Perhaps it's a question of semantics, who knows, but I feel incredibly relieved to be done with "family," "home"—these are things you grow up to leave and be done with, at least as much as school. To claim, as some would, that select human add-ons after the split—a lover or a spouse, say, or bosom buddies, sidekicks, or semi-regular drinking companions (and you'll notice I'm not mentioning offspring)—constitute not only family, but a "purer" version of family based on choice and real need, and that we "all" need family in some configuration . . . I see such assertion as wordplay, I see it as a fucking CROCK.

The first member of my family, my original, actual family, the one I was born into—my so-called "blood" scene—whom I was able to dispense with was my father: dear old Dad. It was impossible, it was frighteningly easy, it was all variety of arcane, jagged, stress-filled whatever, but I did it—though of course I haven't really dispensed with him at all. I've never been able to really talk this out, not by the numbers, let me see if I can 'splain it now . . .

My father is dead, he died, but way before that he *sort* of died, became something quitelike dead, for many intents and purposes, so palpably you could just about put a date on it: two dyings, and which should we count? (At 80 and 40.) And there's maybe even a third dying, a child-size giving up in a *major way*, when he was five, but I wasn't there to see it. We've only got his word for it, and it's hard these days to take anything he said literally, any more than wine dark seas or looking glass ties, or even seriously (more than a speech by Reagan or Bush or Clinton).

Who was he? What was he? Fucking beats *me*.

As I find myself reconstructing things, by the time I was five (and my sister was two) it was clear to my parents that they each lacked the energy, the stamina, the basic wherewithal to deal whole-hog (for more than minutes at a time) with two children. One had been plenty, two was a terrible blunder— whudda ya do? The plan from then on was for my mother (with an assist from *her* mother, who lived with us awhile) to handle my sister, "raise" her, all of that, and my father to handle me. We would all be together, more or less, at mealtime and Christmas and on family outings, but that was it.

My sister, it would turn out, was the lucky one. For me, what the setup meant was the old man had full, unrestricted license to own, operate, supervise, to some degree nurture, but above all manipulate me, lead me by a ring through my goddam nose, and crowd me to the point of suffocation. For the next five-six years, he wouldn't fucking leave me alone.

Of course he LOVED me (and I loved him) and all such nonsense—but that part was maybe the worst of it. A sentimental slob, a '40s romantic in desperate need of a compliant

LOVE OBJECT, he inflicted his ardor on me in direct proportion to what he wasn't getting from his wife, assuring me (as often as not) that *I* was the most important being in his life. A sensitive little prick, I grieved for the guy in his loneliness, enabling him to box me in all the more. (While he wasn't getting his quota of wifelove, I was meantime getting even less in the way of motherlove, although years later, when I asked my sister what that had been like, she said with a giggle, "You didn't miss much.") Those times when his game got to be sooo heavy that I went to the old lady for help—or even a recommendation—she'd tell me what amounted to *Hey, he's just my husband. If you're gonna be FRIENDS with the likes of him, you're on your own, kid.*

What I got from this not ungenerous acquaintance was, hell, he showed me how to draw and paint, well enough that I understood color and perspective by the time I was six, taught me all about dinosaurs and starfish and igneous rocks, read me stories from seminal science-fiction collections, dealt me stamps and coins and *all* my hobbies—every one until rock and roll. He also fed me more bullshit than a captive audience should have to endure.

Like he told me, without my asking, where babies came from when I was only like seven, but he also made sure I knew it was "illegal" to poke around if you weren't married—you'd go to JAIL, he said, and for too many years I actually believed him. (Finally I realized he'd been married a virgin and didn't want me having any more fun than he'd had himself.)

Every weekend, he took me to the movies, something I'd much rather have done with folks my own age. During the 20-block walk to and from the theater, he would deliver a lecture, or a meditation or monologue. En route to *Revenge of the Creature* and *This Island Earth*, he filled me with crap about the terrible Commies (never accept an apple pie from strangers: Communists have been known to lace them with HAIR), then afterwards, as the sun went down, he hit me with a grim blend of science and sci-fi, i.d.'ing clouds, explaining the coloration, and concluding, "This is how it will look at the end of the world." (Say what?)

Above all, he regaled me with tales of his glorious premarital past, like the time he and some pals had been to a NUDIST CAMP—what wild and krazy s.o.b.'s—and this other time (drunk!) they'd swum out to a yacht moored off Sheepshead Bay and spent the night. (How pathetic to hear such hooey—at a moment when his only friend was ME.) In the late '30s, as "press agent" for a semi-pro football team, he allegedly phoned in "game reports" to the *Brooklyn Eagle*. Yet when we watched a game together (before instant replay) and I asked him what a draw play was, all he could say was, "Draw play? I know what a *screen* play is."

A lifetime Democrat, he twice voted for Eisenhower over Stevenson, on the grounds that "Ike was my commanding officer"—yeah, right. In 1940, the story went, he'd joined the army to "save England from the Blitz" (as opposed, more likely, to escape the clutches of *his* unhappy pappy), only to slip on the ice at Fort Ethan Allen, Vermont, tear a cartilage in his knee, and get classified 4-F a year before Pearl. Usually the story was preamble to his long-range plan for keeping "our" military heritage alive: I would sign up for ROTC ("Better to be an officer") when I turned 18. I was in fucking kindergarten when he first served me this scenario, and not a day went by that I didn't cringe at the thought of growing older (subtracting from 18 to figure how many years I had left).

Though the Meltzers as a unit never participated in the rites of any organized religion (other than Postwar Capitalism), Ol' Man Meltz—though it might've just been a *riff*, y'dig?, tossed off in the same manner he read me sci-fi— occasionally fed me passages from the Bible (flaming pits and all), scaring the PISS out of me, and sometimes pretended to still be a Catholic—he'd been one for seven months. In 1935, to join an Irish frat at Brooklyn College—his way of being anything but a Jew—he took vows or whatever you do, ate no meat on Fridays, went to confession—the whole number—for as long as he could keep it up. It was easier to be an Irish Catholic, he surmised, than an Irish drunk. In all the years I knew him, he'd only sip beers and *feign* being drunk—what an actor. (He also collected beer mugs.)

Yet I lived to tell it. As so-called fate would have it, the weight of the whole thing proved too much for the old fuckeroo to continue to bear. When I was ten or eleven, the charade began to unravel. First to go were our trips to the movies. Maybe it was *Creature with the Atom Brain*, maybe *The Creeping Unknown*—something broke the camel's back. One weekend he announced, flat out, that he'd had enough of the shitty flicks we'd been going to—"half baked" was his term—and if I wished to see any more such trash, *he* wouldn't be along for the ride. Huh whuh?—fuck *you*—as if this silly dance was MY idea! At first I felt double-crossed . . . then a feeling of RELIEF set in.

In short order, he threw in the towel on father-son, on family altogether. Though for all appearances he went on behaving pretty much as he had, it was minus the constancy, fervor, commitment. From a simulation of life he moved to a simulation (and a weak one at that) of a simulation. The full cargo of parenting, always a wretched cartoon, is more than *any* adult human, especially in postwar America, should have had to abide (a crack habit seems easier to finesse), and my father (what's the word, lame? a loser? a dork?) was not made for it nohow.

In his labor-intensive—but ultimately finite—run with me, he lacked the killer instinct, strategic foresight, and parental finishing touch to be truly dangerous. If he'd known what he was doing, I'd've become a serial rapist (or a commodities broker) when the dam finally broke. (Call *me* lucky.)

Soon after giving up on the family thing, he gave up, in just as big a way, on Life Itself, even if, in his overachieving whitecollar mode, he probably passed to colleagues as animate for quite a while. No, he didn't give up striving—or even bullshitting—just *caring.*

But with the pressure thus off, and decades to spare, he would still never become someone I (or anyone) could exactly "talk to"—he never mastered smalltalk or became approximately Real. Which today feels sort of tragic—or something—but that's the fucking breaks.

MIDDLE BEGINNING END

MOTHER'S DAY

If you put it in strictly binary terms, not allowing me the luxury of a scale from 0 to 10, and insisted I answer basically a yes-no question, "close" or "not-close," I would have to say my mother and I have never been close, not in any substantive way in this here world, this here life, but I did once have hot, drippy sex dreams about her, one of which, 20-some years ago, led directly to this poem:

well whaddaya know
it's my semi-annual
FUCK MY MOM DREAM
only this time
she is *not* holding back
I am getting to penetrate
to several inches
of penile excitement
her 35-yr-old
luvpit d'amour

is juicy
is it ever juicy
it's got the stuff
she must be on the pill
or the timing is cool or something
'cause she is not diaphragming it tonite
tonite?
no, it's day
—light is streaming in—
my *birth* day (36)
and also *mother's* day
a great day for mom & son alike
mother's day 1952 I was 7
and I went 'n' caught
Lost Continent starring Sid Melton & Cesar Romero
in green & white
the print was tinted green—true
and after that I can't recall if *my* day
and *her* day
were ever the *same* day
never sent her a card
never bought her lace hankies
or a box of chocolate covered
hazel nuts
never gave fuck-all f'r a holiday
you didn't get school off for
mother's day is *not* a holiday
nor is it a holy day
never gave a thimble worth of piss for it

then or now
but this fuck dream I'm having
is developing to where I've eaten her already
fingered her clit from behind her back
she *likes* the finger more than the tongue
but she *does* like the tongue
—I don't think she's faking it—
dick tho she's got less stake in
but *in* it is
it's up her
and throbbing
and ready to spit a healthy mother-load
up mom's golden passage
all the motherlove
I could've bargained for
and jesus did I bargain:
learned square roots when I was 9
long division when I was 3
no actually I was 8
but would've at 3
if she'd've just let me
suck her tit
my mom the math teacher
I was her prize
of the blackboard equation
had pi-r-square up the old wazoo
I'll be Newton before I'm thru
for *you*
you sweet-titted

firm-assed vixen of 35
just a year younger than me
hadda wait I guess
till I was older than you:
you hot blooded
hot young
woman of flesh
and heart
and all that shit including sweat
jeez you've kept me off your pelvis
for centuries mom
but shit ma I'm finally home!
thanx a bunch mom, ain't it great?
your only son
the firstborn fruit of your womb
planting his hot creamy seed
up your real swell
hot steamy CREASE
I *knew* all those logarithms would someday pay off between
    us
rhythms of my log howev
are not exactly
to your liking
you ain't moving no more
I *know* you didn't come
whatsamatter?—
you seem to be bored or somethin'
AND SHE SEZ TO ME:
look I don't like dicks

just don't *like* 'em
I *don't*
so please remove it
I mean if you can get it over with quick, okay
but enough is enough
how much more do I gotta take?
it shrivels
it droops
SHE CONTINUES:
finger me tho I'd kinda like
you can just keep working my clit
that I like
I like it a *lot*
you can eat me if it'd make you happy
but—really—I don't like dicks . . .
she don' like 'em, she don' like 'em
what's a boy to do???
this frustrated sonnyboy
to the bitter end
willingly strokes her
button of love
love for someone
or some dream
or the original Lost Horizon of 1937
—she liked that movie—
but not for me . . .
r-r-ring goes the wake-up call
at the Hi-Way Host Motel on Colorado Boulevard
hard

my real one
not the dream one
is
it's fucking popping:
I got into mom!
if only for a couple secs
that's s-e-C-s not s-e-X-x
jeez the puns in this part of town
're driving me nuts—
whoops there's another one
and nuts not in chocolate
or in a cookie or somethin'
are nuts she can *do without*
just like the funny-lookin'
skin-thing
that shares its name
with the one *she* gave me
Dick . . . ie Meltzer
"Little Dickie" to his friends
4 foot 7 inches of mathematically worthless
unathletic
bookwormish—
hey does he even *have* a dick?
y'know to match his goofy *name*?
not that SHE'd give a flying hoot
either way
dick of any color
talent, shape or face
she don't like dicks singular or plural

and I know in my singular BONE
why I never sent her
flowers

PAST

Imagine not having one.

DEATH

In the four years since I'd last seen her, I'd managed to finally get a FANTASTIC tattoo I'd coveted for probably 50 years, one in which my mother's being (if not her likeness) played a central role, but it seemed a good idea not to show it to her. She was halfway through her 80s, see, and had had a couple of little strokes, not the kind that leave you paralyzed or powerless to control certain bodily functions—hers only, uh, meddled with her memory—but a stroke of any magnitude comes baggaged with allusions to, well, death (hey)—so I figured it wouldn't be right to rub her nose in the damn thing: A TOMBSTONE W/ "MOM."

What a beauty!!!

During my sandy summers in Rock Rock Rockaway Beach, the late '40s, early '50s, I saw some bang-up tattoos on the arms and chests of sailors and hepsters and hoodlums and so forth, hotter 'n' hepper *by far* than those lick-ons they sold in candy stores for a penny a sheet.

There was this guy I saw once with no arms, just stumps, and a state-of-the-art pompadour somebody must've combed for him. On one stump he had an anchor with a snake twined around it—how do I remember this?—and on the other, his mother's headstone with flowers and shit.

This wurn't the first time I eyeballed a mom-stone on somebody's person, nor by any means the last. It was a my-t-popular design back then, an idiomatic discharge of contempo-iconic whatsafugga. Before "cool" entered white mainstream youth parlance, I know that on some visceral level I regarded the design, the icon, as very, very COOL. Don't ask me to explain it (ain't sure I could).

So anyway—hey—flying in to see my living mom, I decided, though it was summer, to keep my sleeves down. If somehow the plan failed, like if I had a beer and it got so hot I inadvertently rolled 'em up and she caught a peek of the good'un on my arm and *said* somethin', I could tell her it was simply a *classic design* from the archives of tattoo yore . . . hey hey! . . . NO REFERENCE to present company intended.

She'd buy that, right?

SMALL TALK

My mother now lives with my sister in, of all places, Woodstock, N.Y. At this stage of things it's *just* a place, not so flagrantly bohemian anymore (if it ever really was), nor artsy in more than a stripmall frou-frou sort of way—a middleclass town like many another, green and white and small, neither rural per se nor wholeheartedly suburban.

Still and all, 'gainst the tide of histories both bogus and real, W*o*o*d*s*t*o*c*k qua *name* lingers on as a buzzword for, well, *you* know.

Which makes this an ironic, and mildly implausible, outcome: that this is the place where my mother lingers on, holed up for the rest of her days, seeing as how she is quite literally the only adult human I know (as opposed to know *of*) who has NEVER SMOKED POT or sought ANY means, for that matter, of getting off. "Consciousness" hasn't been too big a theme in her life, nor has "pleasure" . . . what the hey.

Fortunately there were other things for the old gal and me to talk about, and on the morning following my arrival, after my sister finally found her cassette recorder, we shot the shit . . .

R. Meltzer: So how do you like the view out this window? You ever just sit here and look out?

E. Meltzer: Uhh . . . no. It doesn't really interest me.

RM: Yeah? You'd rather watch television?

EM: I look at television. Or I'll go sit outside in the back.

RM: You ever see a deer go by here?

EM: Uhh . . . not this close. In the other . . . I saw three of them the other day, right there in that . . . uh . . .

RM: In *that* window?

EM: Yeah, yeah.

RM: And you liked that?

EM: Yeah. Nice to *look* at.

RM: But unless there's a deer or something, it's not much of a view?

EM: It's alright. I'm enjoying what's going on with this leaf, this bush here. It's getting bigger, its growth . . .

RM: It's growing towards the window?

EM: Not that, but it's, uh, the bulbs that were there are getting bigger. The little bulbs or whatever you wanna call them.

RM: Buds?

EM: Yeah.

RM: They're gonna blossom? They gonna be flowers?

EM: I don't know. I don't know.

RM: And do you *like* being in this house, in this town?

EM: It's as good a place as any . . . heh heh heh heh heh.

RM: Do you remember living in Florida?

EM: Oh yeah. How do you know that?

RM: I *saw* you in Florida.

EM: Oh really?

RM: Many times.

EM: That was nice, a very nice place to live.

RM: You liked the weather there.

EM: Weather doesn't bother me one way or the other.

RM: I don't think you like things cold.

EM: Well, the weather in Florida would be cold too.

RM: *Could* be once in a while, but not usually.

EM: Well . . . huh.

RM: I remember once I was down there, it was January and there was ice on the ground.

EM: Hmmm.

RM: 29 degrees.

EM: Heh heh heh heh heh.

RM: It was right near your birthday.

EM: When is that?

RM: January 7.

EM: Are you sure of that?

RM: Yes. Do you remember my birthday?

EM: I'm afraid not.

RM: May 10.

EM: May 10?

RM: Yeah, spring.

EM: Huh. How old are you?

RM: I'm 57.

EM: You're a young man.

RM: Young enough.

EM: And do you know how old I am?

RM: You're 86.

EM: About . . . something like that.

RM: And that's young enough too.

EM: Heh heh heh heh.

RM: But these numbers after a while, they get kind of
abstract . . . like what's 57? What's 86?

EM: 57 is young!

RM: Well yeah, thanks.

EM: Heh heh heh heh heh.

RM: So when you watch TV, you have favorite shows?

EM: Not particularly.

RM: I heard you watch *Wheel of Fortune* every day.

EM: *Wheel of Fortune?* Well, that's because that's part of my, after *Jeopardy* is *Wheel of Fortune*.

RM: Ah *ha*. So *Jeopardy* you *like*, and *Wheel of Fortune* you just . . .

EM: Well, *Wheel of Fortune* could be almost anything . . . there is nothing special about it.

RM: It's not much of a show?

EM: No, it's not. It's more of a, a . . . oh, what's his name? I forget.

RM: The guy who hosts the show?

EM: Yeah.

RM: Pat Sajac? Does he still do the show?

EM: Pat Sajac, yeah . . . but not *Wheel of Fortune*.

RM: *Jeopardy?* Alex Trebeck?

EM: No. No.

RM: You're talking about a third show?

EM: No.

RM: A show that's on after *Wheel of Fortune?*

EM: *Jeopardy* is on *before*. It's on at 7 o'clock at night. And *Wheel of Fortune* is on at 7:30 or so.

RM: So you're talking about what's on at 8 o'clock?

EM: No, what's on at 8 . . . I'm in bed by 8. I'm talking about the fellow who's on, the actor who's on at 7:30. I keep forgetting his name.

RM: An actual *actor* who's on *Wheel of Fortune?*

EM: Uh huh.

RM: You don't mean Vanna White.

EM: No. There's a fellow who's on . . .

RM: Well I don't watch it, I don't know.

EM: Hmmm.

RM: So wait, you watch *those*, but what about before *Jeopardy*, 6:30—is there a show on before that you . . .

EM: No.

RM: Just those two, and then you fall asleep?

EM: At 8 o'clock I go to sleep.

RM: How come you're so noncommittal when I ask you whether you like these shows?

EM: Well, during the week *Jeopardy* and *Wheel of Fortune* are on every night, y'know, not the weekend but . . .

RM: But do you like them or not like them?

EM: Oh yes, I do. I'm just trying to think of the name of the actor.

RM: Well, tonight I'll watch it with you and we'll see.

EM: Heh heh heh heh heh.

SHOWTIME

Alex Trebeck. Pat Sajac. Vanna White. That's it.

No other actors or faces or nothin'. And the kicker was she had no recollection of having brought it up. Gone from the files: phffff.

Heh heh heh heh heh.

But her mind was alert, and quick, quick enough. She even guessed some of the dumb word things on *Wheel of Fortune*.

Maybe watching this shit five nights a week is *good for her*.

A DAY I REMEMBER CLEAR AS DAY

More'n half a century ago. Truman is President. A weekday afternoon, cold blue sky, the winter sun lost behind a row of buildings, walking freezy side streets with my mother and sis.

No more than three-four blocks from where we live, yet somehow, seemingly, we've never been this way before. Maybe it's only our vector of approach, the sights and sight-lines at this particular hour, or the fact that not another soul is in view, but this is unfamiliar, daunting turf for us—a bleak deserted landscape of stucco houses, bungalows, dark shadows and dust.

Daunting and also invigorating . . . *thrilling*.

My 2-year-old sister is in the stroller I used to ride in, hard brown molded plastic, all bundled up, very little skin exposed. Our faces red from the cold. So very unlikely for the three of us to be out together . . . a rarity I'm relishing . . . but enough walk, we're freezing, time to get home.

I spot this alley—a short cut, let's take it!—but my mother has no interest. A dingy walkway where we'd have to go single file . . . too much of a "boy thing"—if I want it, I'm on my own. Fine by me: 's gotta be the first time she's let me *be* on my own, even this close to home, without some version of supervision—without a leash. Yippee yay!

So I race down the alley, one block, another—hey, I'll show *her*, I'll beat 'em home!—and then suddenly a dog barks, *roars*, this hairy beast lunging at a chain-link fence to my left, and I burst into tears and dash back where I came from.

By the time I'm on the main street again, out of breath, my cheeks stinging from the tears, my mom and sis ain't in sight . . . fuggit. In the same instant I feel both betrayed—abandoned!—and hugely embarrassed . . . gotta collect myself *quick* to avoid HUMILIATION. I wipe my face with a mitten and walk briskly, too breathless to run. They'll beat me home, but maybe not by much.

As I stomp along, heart pounding, I know—know!—my mom would not have gone back to look for me, not in finite time. I know she will never participate with me in boy things—in *my* things—my energy and brand o' mischief (what a filthy, yukky alley!!) ain't for her. I feel absolutely alone— she is not my friend nohow. I choke down a thudding gulp of insecurity—she might not've come back to SAVE MY LIFE.

But these thoughts take a back seat to the SCREAMING URGENCY of the moment: to get home pronto and *pretend nothing happened.* Don't want my mother to see me as a scaredy-cat, nor do I want her to know I encountered d-d-danger—she might never let me out again.

Whether there have been precursors to this moment or not, THIS is the defining episode, the fount of all Et Cetera, I will forever revisit. From this day forth, skittish and unloved, I will play the little tough guy, tough to myself at least, on my own in a big scary world, even a few square blocks' worth of one, a world in which monsters in alleys will always lunge at me . . . so I'd better watch my ass.

Without actual friends yet, I'll be on my own in spades. If I venture anywhere, it will be without an ally, a helping hand, even a second opinion. What *is* a friend? I wonder (*where* do I find one?).

And then, whoops, next thing I know, a friend comes calling . . . only—DANGER! DANGER!—that "friend" is my hapless daddy-o.

OLD MAN MELTZ

Pompous blowhard; stultifying omnipresence; dreary s.o.b. with a heart of gold, no, silver, no, aluminum; white collar drudge; earnestly mawkish drip-dry sap.

SOMEBODY ELSE'S O.M.

By the time I got around to having one drilled in my arm, the vogue for tombstone tattoos, honoring mothers or brothers or anybody, had been gone with the wind for *decades*.

In the late '60s, you could still walk into most any tattoo joint in the country and get a sampling of headstone/gravesite designs, two or three or four, different eras, different artists, the real deal. Through the '70s and '80s, the frequency declined steadily, and on the brink of the new millennium, in the 10–12 joints where I peeped at the wares, there were NONE. Not on walls, in portfolios or display books, nor in dusty file cabinets . . . nothin'. Oh, well.

Finally I met this kid named Cherokee, a tattoo apprentice whose father had once been B-b D- - -n's heroin dealer, and over the next few months he designed me a *lulu*. Stone-cutter lettering . . . jagged, "weathered" edges . . . symmetrically petaled fleurs to the left and right . . . fat, fleshy blades o' grass, lotsa grass (hence lotsa green) . . . lookin' good!

To which, per my request, he added a woman's hand groping upward from the sod. (She's hard to *keep under*, y'see.)

POLYPS

Quick! What were you doing the day, the moment, you first heard "Surfin' Safari"?

That's easy. I was in a '55 Merc with my parents & sister headed for Horace Harding Hospital, Queens, N.Y., so my mother could have surgery to remove a polyp. September '62. A Monday.

But the kinda polyp, *that* I don't remember. Nor does my mother. Nor my sis.

My father? He don't 'member *nothin'*. He's dead.

SAFETY FIRST

Tho responsible for the bulk of *emotional* mayhem round the house, and all too adept at tormenting & badgering me in arcane, labyrinthine ways, my father was uncomfortable with physical intimidation, and his forays into corporal discipline/punish were fiascos. High-strung, he'd end up hitting himself 'stead of me—scary shit—but on a couple of occasions, when I was 6 or so, *totally* losing it over who fucking knew what, he actually took shots at me, with his hand and a rolled up science-fiction mag. Weak swats to the butt, they were painless but jarring just as morbid accelerations of a woebegone psyche.

My mother, on the other hand, cool (let's even call her cold), not given normally to weird takeoffs or landings, once WALLOPED me with staggering unrestraint—in the face no less—to stop me from LAUGHING.

Could we call the lady prudent? A Chesterfield smoker her whole growed-up life, she gave up cigs forever, cold turkey, the minute the Surgeon General came out with his first big announcement about, y'know, cancer and what-all . . . didn't even give herself a final puff.

No fan of vermin or boystuff, she barely noticed the crawling & flying things imprisoned in lidded jelly jars around my room. A hobby she left me alone with—fat city. I was so stoked, tho, from capturing my first black widow that I went 'n' showed her the shiny little fugger—"Look! The hourglass!"—whereupon she dumped and squooshed it with a patent leather slipper shinier than the spider. Good thing I didn't mention I'd found it in the basement, in a web alongside this enormous egg case, or we'd ALL have got cancer from the oceans of pesticide she'd've bombed the house with.

Okay, so nobody got bit and kilt by the 8-legged spouse eater (possible assist to *her*). But this laugh caper, *sheez*—heck hath no fur like a mom who CARES . . .

Ralph and Ed were mixing their first test batch of the hair restorer they'd been flammed into buying a boatload of, investing their pitiful savings to get!rich!quick! or in any case get the bloody hell out of Bensonhurst. Kramden and Norton—the male half of *The Honeymooners*.

Ed reads the label on one bottle: "H20."

Ralph corrects him: "Those in the know just call it *ho*."

Ed, being Ed, gets a little sloppy. "Watch it, Norton! Don't spill that ho like it was water!"

Being in the ho-know myself, a precocious 9-year-old math & science simp, I *exploded*. One of those goddam PAROX-YSMS you feel in your gut like you're doing situps or something, hoowooooo! . . . body-mind *intensity* like I wouldn't experience otherwise till I started fucking.

So my mother sees me spasm-ing like some crazy toy, having the time of my life!—joyous in my own skin—and what does she do, she hauls off and slugs me.

She was a textbook person, ya dig, and according to the book—whichever one—such a brutal response was not merely the safe thing but the ONLY thing to do. Mandatory!

Laughter can be perilous bizness, apparently. Who *knows* what mighta-coulda happened if I'd kept it up?

Cryin' to keep from laughin'!

What dizzy backwards dawg-shit.

THE SETUP

RM: Do you cook anymore?

EM: I haven't cooked in a long time. I do make, y'know, I'll make bagels and I'll cook, every morning I cook a bagel and that's my breakfast.

RM: Do you remember when you used to cook . . .

EM: I guess I used to cook.

RM: . . . these elaborate recipes for . . .

EM: That was a long time ago. A long time ago.

RM: You used to get these recipes from *Woman's Day*, *Family Circle*.

EM: You're talking about me?

RM: Yes. Things with names like Chicken Almondine.

EM: Heh heh heh.

RM: Which was like chicken with slivered almonds, the kind that're already slivered in the package.

EM: Huh.

RM: And you also did various Chinese dishes, like fried rice and um, I think you got that off the Minute Rice box.

EM: Mmm hmm. How about you? Do you do cooking of any kind?

RM: Oh, I don't make things that are very complicated, but I cook for myself and I . . . well, once in a while I'll make my own pasta sauce, y'know, from mushrooms, peppers, that kind of thing.

EM: Huh.

RM: But usually I'll just, I'll use a jar of sauce and add my own spices. I'm trying to mainly eat *healthier* food than I've been eating.

EM: Good.

RM: I eat very little meat.

EM: So are you gonna try and eat *more* meat?

RM: No no, I was eating *too* much meat.

EM: Oh?

RM: So now I don't eat much meat at all.

EM: Oh.

RM: And instead, y'know . . . fish, chicken . . . vegetables. I never liked salads when I was growing up, but now I do.

EM: Salads I've always liked.

RM: I liked what we ate last night at that restaurant.

EM: What we ate?

RM: When we went out to that restaurant.

EM: We did?

RM: You had ravioli, you remember the ravioli?

EM: I didn't have ravioli.

RM: Yes you did. You had ravioli, and there were these strange-shaped mushrooms that you couldn't figure out . . .

EM: What it was.

RM: . . . immediately . . . but we figured out, looking at the menu, that it was mushrooms.

EM: Heh heh heh.

RM: And I had scallops, and everybody else at the table had *steaks*.

EM: I didn't have steak?

RM: No.

EM: I don't trust mushrooms. I'll eat them, but I don't trust them.

THE PUNCHLINE

I always had a hunch that Esther B. Meltzer had never breast-fed me. It just seemed like . . . she hadn't. At 49 or 50, I finally got around to asking her.

"Of course not. Nobody did in those days."

"But lots of women must've done it once or twice—just to see what it felt like."

"Not me."

"You weren't even curious?"

"Absolutely not!" Well, okey doke.

Not much of a nurturer, if truth be told, she also wasn't much of a cook.

"Fresh" and "ripe" were v. low on her agenda. For every fresh apricot or peach, we had canned or frozen a dozen times, regardless of the season. There wasn't a single fresh mushroom in my entire childhood. We never had fresh peas. Never a soup made from ingredients, only canned or boxed. Never a pear that wasn't hard as a rock.

Her attempts at salad were minimalist nightmares. Lettuce/celery/tomato was the basic deal, no onion (we only got onions on burgers). Her tomatoes of choice were cellophane-wrapped hardballs so wooden they might take weeks to ripen, and she never waited a day. It's a wonder her knives could cut them. Dressing was some variable (but ever insipid) ratio of vinegar to mayonnaise. Fortunately, she only attempted these a couple times a year.

Potatoes she didn't hafta wait on to ripen, but still you gotta *do something* with 'em, and Esther had verylittle aptitude for spuds. Home fries, fat-fried scalloped, whatever you wanna call 'em, were a slimy, undercooked mess, and mashed were a triple dare (boil, mash and spice) she shoulda politely declined.

Basically, she didn't—on a first-name basis—know a spice besides salt. They were there in the cupboard, sure, part of some official '50s "homemaker" thing, she just never used them. In my early teens, I took to spicing up the meat-loaf when she wasn't lookin', mixing in garlic, pepper, thyme, paprika 'fore it went in the oven—half an act of mischief, half one of survival. (Her own palate not being attuned to the parameters of such ado, she failed to notice the diff.)

The mix-&-match of main course and condiment: chicken w/ ketchup!! How *else* to cover up the greezy gristly BLAND of it all? Steak sauce mighta worked, but we never had steak sauce. Chicken Almondine—why'd I *flatter* her?—had tinfoil stuck to it that you hadda scrape off or like *die* or something.

I have NEVER et a hamburger more vile than my mother's. I retch every time I think of one.

But nowhere as bad as whenever I think of her slime-baked frozen mackerel ... *yikes*. There was no cover-up sauce, and no lemon when you needed one, only ReaLemon in a bottle (before they had the squeeze-thing). Pretty rancid stuff ... "fishy" in its most diz-gusting incarnation. I grew up HATING fish and FEARING it.

But her gag-reflex masterpiece had to be her GRILLED CHEESE SALTINES. Squares of Velveeta 'tween Nabisco saltines were sizzled and tortured in an inch of Wesson oil, saturating the cracker till you could see the cheese through it. Spatula'ed from the pan, they were drained on paper towels which became stinky enormous GREASE MATS. Two of these treats were enough to destroy any hunger. I can't remember my sister or me ever eating more.

Great moments in killing your kids!

MY LIFE AS A PENIS

I came home from the last day of kindergarten without a report card. "The teacher didn't call my name," I explained. The last name, yeah, but not the first: no Dickie, only a certain *Richard* Meltzer—whoever the fuck *he* was.

"Richard is your real name," my mom was obliged to admit. "Dickie is your *nickname*." Say whuh?

The way it worked till then was she'd arranged with my teacher to call me Dickie in class, but that day there was a substitute, and what the dootz did *she* know?

Aw well, I'll live, I figured.

Then, in second grade, I discovered that dick = penis . . . jesus f. *christ*. I lobbied the parents to stop nicking me and go real already—"Call me Richard"—but it was like pulling teeth. (Not for another ten years—symbolically enough: the day I graduated high school—did they agree in principle to accede to my request. My father began *trying* to call me Richard . . . it took my mother ten more to even begin.)

In the meantime, for the remainder of my childhood, I kept my eyes open for what today you would call role models. Richard the Lionhearted I knew was *bullshit*. Some Brit named Richard Greene played Robin Hood on TV—but he wasn't Robin Hood, he was an *actor*. Finally, a few months after catching Elvis on *Ed Sullivan*, I saw this flick called *Mister Rock and Roll*, and dig it dig it DIG IT: Little Richard!

Who leered and smirked and yawped and yowped and surged and manifested BIG HUNKS of previously unrevealed Universe and *got down*.

And was so goddam palpably REAL.

Which turned out to be a good deal, I guess. If not for my predickament, heh, and my predicament writ large, i.e., small, Little Richard might not've had quite the impact on me that he did.

I was a little guy myself, y'know, on the cusp of adolescence. Suddenly having Richard Penniman as my psychic co-pilot made me two-thirds, at least, of all I would ever be—or need to be—Richardwise.

Sometimes you luck the fuck out.

MUSIC! MUSIC! MUSIC!

My father had a "thing" for Hawaiian music, or said he did, yet I never heard him play any, on records or radio, in all the years I lived with him. The only music he paid active attention to, tunes of the '50s and early '60s passing through the ether, was the occasional hit evincing the theme "Life is grief." Weepers like Bobby Vinton's "Roses Are Red" ("Is that your little girl? She looks a lot like you") and Kitty Kallen's "My Coloring Book" ("Color me blue") affected him *viscerally*. So would perennials like the Bing Crosby "White Christmas" or any version of "Danny Boy." He always got mushy over Eddie Fisher's "Oh My Papa," not so much because it clicked him back to his own papa, but 'cause he wished and hoped I would feel the same buzz of sentiment for mine.

To my mother, meanwhile, music, current or ancient, meant virtually NOTHING. The original cast album from

South Pacific, the LP heard most often in our home, was but a keepsake of the Broadway show, of her memorable journey with my father to Manhattan, dinner at Rosoff's, etc., etc.— an evening she talked about for *years*—but one without enduring *sonic* specificity. Even when her memory was more or less intact, she couldn't've passed a blindfold test for "Some Enchanted Evening."

My father *objected* to rock & roll (it rattled his, y'know, world). My mother never even noticed it.

DRAGONS

My sister first became aware that "something" was a little off with our mom when she took her to some silly movie about knights and dragons and such hoke, and on the way out the momperson said, "Those were the days . . . back when dragons still existed."

When I heard this, it struck me as kind of endearing . . . childlike. If she was losing anything, I said, it was all these useless layers of sophistication. Here she was back at a place of open-eyed innocence—what could be wrong with that?

No, Nancy insisted, there was nothing that sweet about it. Here was the loss of a frigging faculty: something *functional*. That she didn't *remember* there ain't never been dragons was, fuh, a verybad sign.

Well since then the losing has picked up speed, and I can see with my own eyes things fallin' away like Post-Its in a wind tunnel . . . whatever, that is, that hain't already fallen.

She doesn't remember her lousy cooking or her horrible driving or the fact that she smoked or taught trigonometry, nor does she actually remember her husband anymore—hasn't mentioned him since her daughter stopped showing pics of him—and it troubles me now that I can't recall certain things about her either.

Like her smell, for inst.

There were so few hugs, so little close-quarters contact, that I have absolutely no sense recollection of the odor, the fragrance, of her flesh.

If the house hadn't reeked of tobacco and foodstink, maybe I'd've picked up whiffs of her without the hugs . . . dunno. All I know is this: I don't rightnow remember how she smelled, nor am I clear on whether I *ever* knew it. I just can't for the life of me scare up a take on how she might even *theoretically* have smelled when I was young and she was (yes yes) the v. first object of my hot-dang desire.

SCENT OF A GEEZER

My second morning in Woodstock, when I joined her on the porch, my mother smelled like chocolate donuts and shampoo. We sat for 30–40 minutes and she listened intently as I wheeled out old stories, mundane and not, trying (I suppose) to see if she remembered anything about anything, stuff like aunts and cousins and our beat-up old house and dinky little town and grade school and the beach and actors and actresses she used to like.

With infectious good cheer, she'd say things like "You have a great memory!"—trusting me implicitly—"I don't remember *any* of that," then shift to doubt mode—"You're not kidding me, are you?"—then back again.

Finally she asked: "But how do you *know* all these things?"—like how could I, a stranger, be privy to so damn much?

"Well, except when I went off to college, I lived with you till I was 21."

"Really? Do you know my son Richard?" Geez—what a classic straight line. Could she be kidding *me*?

"You're looking at him."

"No!"

"*I'm* Richard."

"Heh heh heh heh heh heh heh heh!" Real laughs, not nervous titters. What a comedy team!

She just seemed so AMAZED in the nicest way, pleased to learn I was her son—after knowing damn well who I was yesterday and the night before. The double-edged "revelation" (BLOOD, y'know, and FORGETTING) didn't especially alarm either of us, 'cause it felt kind of in a way *irrelevant* . . . we were otherwise getting along so well, y'know?

THE LIFE OF MY PENIS IN
A WORLD WITHOUT SEX

My first sightings of scumbags, as they prob'ly still call them back east—"bags" for short—were of *used* scumbags in various states of decomposition, tossed in the street by horny hepcats,

I presumed, on the rebound from red-hot rock-roll sexdates, a grace note to their evening which said, "Hey, I got some!"—like *wow*. Seeing them in the gutter beside a cigarette butt, on somebody's lawn, or under a bus stop bench got me all tingly with idiot expectancy: someday *I* would get some too.

First time I saw a fresh, unused scumbag was in summer camp. Jerry the counselor took one out of this gold coin-shaped case, unrolled it to its full extension, waved it over his head—what a card—re-rolled it. Hey, Jerry got *plenty*.

The first bag I actually handled came out of a 36-box of Trojans I found in my father's sock drawer. Three dozen—what wishful thinking. In the two years I kept checking, the count never got below the mid 20s. My folks didn't fuck much, see. I never heard things *remotely* like fucksounds or bouncy bedsprings.

Why waste good bags? If they weren't being used, might as well put 'em on my own wiener, OK? Every so often, if I got hard, I'd roll one over my thing and tug on it a little, then put it back. Unlubricated, basic boring white latex—but what'd *I* know? It all seemed pretty magical to me.

This was before I'd ever even jerked off, eh, and the first time I tugged it all the way, came and everything (whoopee), lookin' at pics in a mag that didn't show nipples or cunthair or complete naked butts, no skin but cleavage and thighs, I *by design* wore one of these communal Trojans. It seemed the classy way to go—doin' it like you would if you were *really fucking*. That one I didn't put back in the box.

Hey. There was lotsa good wacky sexual energy in the house, but the only ADULT sex energy you could feel in the air was my father's lumbering frustration . . . fluggit.

Here was this poor lusty guy, one of whose REASONS for marrying was to get some ginch (didn't seem to 've known how to score any w/out), and he still wasn't getting it. Was the impasse a "chemistry" thing? Dunno, but it was a lucky day when he even copped a *kiss* off the missus (more of that naughty boystuff). Lotsa times she shoved him off for getting too close. I would bet the FARM they never ate each other.

Oh, d'I tell you my mom was *really* a hotte-looking woman? In glossies from back then she's Bess Myerson with an *edge*—a curvycurvy 90th-percentile mid-century brunette. Her ev'ryday wardrobe flaunted her niftiest hotwoman features—paraboloid knockers and a *dandy* spherical ass—nifty enough to have helped her "land a husband," whether or not, once the accessories (home, hearth, offspring) had been provided, she deemed it any longer nec. to hop to the promise implied by the flaunt.

A thought just occurred to me that possibly didn't then. Could he have fucked her with one of the bags I tried on myself? Popped his cork way up her forbidden cranny with the lingering AURA of my dick surrounding his own suffer-meat?

Interesting thought!

THE MATH WE DO FOR LOVE

Dirty mags weren't the only paper products I from time to time had to sneak past Esther. She would get on these periodic kicks where comic books were if not outright forbidden, then heavily discouraged, *hah*, and not only stuff like EC, y'know, horror comics and murder and mayhem and all that. Even bland pap like Casper and Disney—Goofy and Pluto and Chip 'n' Dale, those luvable chipmunks—hadda be smuggled in under my shirt and stashed deep somewhere in my room . . . deeper than the old man's condoms.

The way candy was supposed to ruin your appetite for official sit-down meals, a familiarity with comics of any sort, she believed, would terminate the growth of *good reading habits*, i.e., a hunger & craving for hard litrachoor.

"I wish you would read SHAKESPEARE," she told me more than once, which in hindsight is funny and sad and truly absurd. She was not in the slightest a liberal arts pantheon-of-culture type person—who was she kidding?—she taught high school fucking math. The hardest lit she read was Earl Stanley Gardner, Agatha Christie—that and *Reader's Digest*. Mysteries to her were the pulp equivalent of math—problem solving—just like riddles and mazes and how-many-things-are-wrong-with-this-pic?

Well, I didn't fall for the Shakespeare ruse, but I fell for a *major* shitload. To win this woman's love, to stand a chance of even getting on the waiting list, I had to lift boulders with my fingers, elephants with my tongue. I had to acquire a life's worth of academic mettle and muscle by the time I was 7 and keep it up!, keep it up!, for one fucking interminable haul. From first grade onward, college was my destination and destiny, and woe was uh me.

Whew. I was the only kid in town with TWO parents who'd been to college, which woulda been pressure enough, but Mrs. M, more than mere cheerleader and motivator, ran me through the paces like Woody Hayes or George S. Patton. I by all means "got" my work ethic, my discipline, from her, well, from both of them—but she wasn't keen on my father's slob version. Every bit as disciplined—*fuck* yeah—as she would ever be, he was also a grumbler and too, too sweaty a guy. What she demanded amounted to stoicism, to unreflected humdrum—1–2–3–4, do the task—with no mammal content. Plan it . . . do it . . . almost military.

I strapped mind and body to the grindstone and over-achieved like a *motherfucker* (sorry, no pun). She wants 100 on every test? OK, I'll get 100 on every test. Got 'em till every other kid hated my guts. Worked instead of played till I dropped. Carried a schoolbag too heavy for somebody twice my size, one of those hideous giveaways that you're totally useless, without a life, an oofus with no age-peer smarts, and less street sense than a Disney chipmunk.

And what I gained in the transaction, hell, I barely got a hearty handshake. I earned the privilege, basically, of staying at the grindstone in perpetuity.

A perpetuity I ain't shook yet.

Even after she didn't teach it no more, math remained the acme and the ajax of my mother's educational paradigm. I won my high school math medal, some stupid little blue & red thing (a round of claps, please), but by the time I finally entered college, having placed easily into sophomore calculus, I'd had enough of math and its bloodless abstraction. Within a year, following a D in one advanced course and an F in another, I changed my major to philosophy. My mother was *pissed*, and she was no less pissed when, three years later, I got expelled from graduate school, still a philo major.

Grad school? . . . sheeeez . . . I stayed *way* too long in school. I mega-schooled my ass so thoroughly, so indelibly, it feels at times I've never left that wretched giggle-pit. At least once a month, I have a dream where I gotta take a test in some subject I haven't thought about in 40 years—French, let's say. I tell the teacher: "Hey mamzelle, don't fuck with me. I already got an A—I *graduated* this dump!—in 1962."

Then she says: "No matter. You will take THIS test NOW."

"Well, I won't."

"Then we'll take your diploma away."

"Take it!"

"Sorry. You *still* must take the test."

Meaning, I dunno . . . whatever.

All I know is I've been out of school since LBJ was prez, and I'm still dreaming this hogwash. And every time I dream it, I think: it's HER doing.

My loving mom's.

KILL

The faintest of alarms went off, so I went and checked, and sure enough. On page 88 of *The Night (Alone)*, my '95 novel, the guy I've got as my first-person stand-in casually mentions his first tattoo, and what the hey, it's exactly the one I've been telling y'about, well, minus a hand coming out of the earth. Mentions he got it in '69, same year I got *my* first (a shark), and I'm wondering if when I wrote it I felt, in retrospect, that I *should've* got the other one first . . . that's one mem'ry I can't shake loose.

But, god, thoughts of this tat have been with me a *long-long* time, and I'm still achin' for an angle on what, um, might underlie the funereal fixation. Maybe this: That while my father, for all his twitchy incompetence, was too appalling to imagine killing, too pathetic to even picture dead, my mother, for all her cold, sassless dominion, was a relative pushover. ONE of 'em had to go . . . so let it be her.

Kill the mother: Now I am a man? Wasn't that Freud's puppy? Or was it Bruno Bettelheim's?

Henry Rollins'?

OKLAHOMA CITY

My father's been dead eight years. He died very grimly. I don't wanna die like he died.

Nine years before, he'd been diagnosed with Parkinson's, but he began slipping into the fog long before that. Was he already "senile"—that déclassé catchall? How 'bout "feeble"? "Demented"? Well, certainly one or all of the above.

When the diagnosis came in, my mother's response was "Oh, that *explains it.*" While it failed to supply full specificity for his physical-emotional-existential "condition," it at least opened a window on how fucked-up he was. Now that *something* was finally official, she had valid reason, thank *both* their lucky stars, to treat him as a SICK PERSON and administer compassion in doable (if largely medicinal) doses. Before that, she dealt with him as some kind of reprobate, a slacker when it came to the usual homestead grunt-work, scolding him for goofing off when all he was doing was shivering terrified in the fog.

Possibly I exaggerate the severity of her disapproval—it maybe wasn't quite that severe, nor all that consistent—but until his proper-noun malady became one of *her* designated chores, she was anything but kind to him.

During the last couple years of his life, he could rarely get food down without ordeal. Nose drool dribbled down his face much of the day. He dislocated a shoulder. Couldn't wipe his own butt, and wore diapers. When he wasn't in bed, strapped in tight, he was strapped into a wheelchair, the placement of which was well beyond his control.

With about 6 months to go, a doctor estimated the ol' guy to be "no more than 5 percent conscious," and it took tremendous effort to crank him up in the morning, to try and get him to utter a word or two, to express anything (one way or another) about zip. In lieu of aiming to trigger such a payoff, what my mother did was simply wheel him in front of the TV and leave the room.

TV! TV! . . . oh boy . . . which for his final week on earth meant that fright show, the Oklahoma City bombing. TV Mom thought NOTHING of having him sit 'n' die before replays of bodies and rubble and symphonized horror, day unto woeful day, hour after hour. The medium is f'r goddam sure the message, and this message in extremis was her final gift to him, the decisive flavoring of his final agony.

Yes, by gum, she did indeed wipe his ass and spoonfeed him purées of pablum and bathe and clothe him and toil above and beyond the call of grunt-work just to keep him alive . . . but really, folks, wouldn't you expect something an itty bit more *personal* in her manner of dealing with HIM, her mate of 51 years—in her mode of communicating and communing with what remained of that itty bit that wasn't yet putrefied bio-matter: the 5 percent, whatever? She never, on evidence, tried to *mingle* with the 5; she gave up, probably, when it was closer to 50.

Hey, people, I hold none of this shit "against" her (honest), but gee, heck, *I* would expect more.

She could at least have rented the video of *Lost Horizon.*

SISTER, BROTHER, SON

Proper nouns with faces, or at least *contexts*. Not too many left.

Esther. Nancy. Lenny. Jessie. Richard. Artie.

Aside from herself, and my sister and her husband and their daughter, and me when her recall is firing on enough cylinders—and hey, throw in Alex, Vanna and Pat—the only other character/role/person, living or dead, who with any frequency comes linked in my mother's front-burner mind with a NAME is her retired pharmacist brother.

Though it isn't clear whether she actually *remembers* Artie anymore, she does get a lotta play out of namedropping him. During one of our Woodstock dialogues, she asked me: "Are you Richard or Artie?"—it hadda be one or the other (we're the two absentees in the lineup). I've seen the guy—a beefy 6-foot bruiser (to my mother's 5-zero)—only once in the last 35 years, and she hasn't seen him in about 10, but even without being fed his photo (Nancy's no fan of our uncle), she still manages to get a great big BUZZ from reciting his name and perhaps (on some level) thinking—or at least *conceiving*—of him.

Which, speaking of photos, might for all we know be more'n can be said about *me*. Without my li'l sis show-&-telling my pic umpteen times a month, who knows if I'd even be half of the Richard-Artie namedrop tag team? (Artie's been a player 50 percent longer'n I have, y'know?) Nancy, at any rate, has been taking no chances, and strut out my mugshots she does. Maybe it's a "sister-brother thing"—and so the hell is Esther-Artie—what's it all fucking ABOUT, eh? But yes, Nancy is a Good Sister (much better, prob'ly, than I am a brother), and on the third day of my stay she made me a nametag for Esther to see:

"RICHARD MELTZER"—first name and last. It gave me an odd feeling to wear it. Even back when she unequivocally knew, I.D.-wise, who I was, she never knew or especially cared who I actually *was*, or *what* I was, y'know what I *did*. I always had this chilly sense that her take on me was more or less "Your son's name goes here." Her regard for me seemed not so much conditional as one-size-fits-all—or an extra-large that itself could never be shaped by the wearer. Beyond my academic record and other markers of the Great Nuthin', she had virtually no interest in the workings of my soul or any but the shallowest details of my non-generic life. For years, I sent her copies of all my books, and she always behaved as if, y'know, proud of me, but she never ever opened one.

Well, shoot—I've never known who the hell she is either.

3RD PERSON

A miscellany of E. Meltzer speculation, interpretation:
Practicality to the point of heartlessness.
Insensitivity without callousness.
Intelligence without awareness or comprehension.
Comfort without enjoyment.

All pleasure as overridingly mental, not to mention methodical: the mastering of mental challenges.

Never just doodled or goofed off. No gratuitous activity of any sort.

Big on accepting the hand-as-dealt, not going against the grain . . . why waste time complaining? But when the complaint is hers . . . uh oh. Throw out the deck and deal again.

Emotional reticence? Self-control? Are unexpressed feelings bottled up—contained and controlled—or merely concealed . . . or are they (possibly) *not even there?* (An unanswerable question.)

2ND PERSON

"Mommy."

'Fore I was 10, I was already having trouble calling her that, and soon it became "Mom." Midway through high school, I began addressing her without any capital M-word at all ("you" seemed perfectly adequate).

These days, when I speak to my sister, I can't bring myself to use such wds. even in a 3rd-person way. Usually it's "How's our mother doing?"—ho ho ho (fuck *me*).

The mommy ROLE I have no trouble with. It's applying it to my own m-person that gives me the heeby jeebs.

"I want my mommy"—*that* number—eeyowwww. She ain't delivered on anything like it in 50-somethin' years.

Hey, I'll cop to it: I *do* want my mommy—*a* mommy (or equivalent). Wish the hell I had one—what the fucking fuck.

TABLE DANCER

So I'm sipping a beer and my mother is sitting there giving me this squinty, not exactly thirsty look, and I ask her, "You want a slug?"

"No thank you."

"You sure?"

"Yes. Did I ever drink beer?"

"No. And you didn't drink wine either. Just whiskey."

"Whiskey?"

"Well, mixed drinks, cocktails, y'know, Manhattans, whiskey sours . . . "

"Really?"

". . . brandy Alexanders . . . "

"I don't believe it!"

"You even got drunk once."

"You're not trying to trick me?"

"I can't trick *you*."

"Heh heh heh heh."

I wasn't there, so who knows what actually happed, but 10 years ago at a wedding, according to Nancy, our female parent not only got looped but made a wildcrazy spectacle of herself.

As implausible as it sounds, she somehow downed five or six more silly geezer drinks than her normal max, *one*, kicked off her shoes, and climbed up and DANCED ON A TABLE-TOP. Work out, Essie!—firs' time in this LIFE she ever let it rip!—but she DIDN' REMEMBER A MINUTE OF IT.

An amnesia variation slightly diff from the current installment . . . and when told the nex' day what a swell time she'd had, she shook her head, tut-tutted gravely, and vowed *never to do it again.*

THE USES & ABUSES OF OBLIVION

No, I'm not gonna trick her, but my sister has, and it's a *good'un.*

Nancy's feet get sore, she's on them a lot, running 'round doing things for the mom (for inst), so finally she tells her: "When I was a little girl and my feet hurt, you rubbed them for me"—an outright lie—"and it always felt so good, so loving. Couldja, wouldja do that now?" And she complied! Does it most days 'pon request!

And Nance ain't the only one to benefit from someone's memory problems. The old gal herself recently got through a traumatic day at the doctor's by losing track of the sequence of big/little past-tense traumas, thus avoiding being traumatized *cumulatively*. She had some node kind of thing, and they had to biopsy it and poke her and ultrasound and bloodsuck her, and all sorts of dire etc., but as minutes became half-hours, even quarter-hours, she would only remember the most micro-immediate horror, and by the time my sister got her home she remembered none of it . . . "Did we just go somewhere?"

So misery-efficient, this life. But if past mis'ries would only just drift away . . . what a deal!

LOVE AND LAUGHTER, EVER AFTER

Fun and games time. On the last day of my visit, I flunk a one-on-one comparison w/ a two-year-old photo. "This is *my* son—you don't look as good as him" . . . fuckit, lady.

Ten minutes later, I take off my nametag and point to its absence on my shirt.

RM: Who am I? Who do you think I am?
EM: You can be anything you want. I don't know who you want to be.

RM: No, I'm not asking you to use your imagination. I'm asking you who I am *in fact*.

EM: Heh heh heh heh heh.

RM: Do you remember *who I am*?

EM: I can't remember the name.

RM: Well, I had a nametag here, I took it off. Do you remember what it said?

EM: . . . . .

RM: Not Artie . . . begins with an R.

EM: Richard . . . Meltzer.

RM: Right!

EM: That's what it is?

RM: That's who I am.

EM: Heh heh.

RM: So you remember.

EM: Richard Meltzer.

RM: It's like you remembered the *nametag*, but not the face that went with it.

EM: Oh yeah?

RM: You didn't think I looked like the guy in the photo.

EM: No . . . heh heh heh.

RM: And why not?

EM: You look *better*.

RM: Oh—before you told me I looked worse.

EM: Heh heh heh heh heh heh heh.

RM: So in other words, I'm your *son*, right?

EM: Right, okay.

RM: It's okay? I'm okay as a son?

EM: Sure you are. Sure you are.

RM: Yeah?

EM: So what?

RM: It's nice to *see* you, y'know, 'cause you're my *mother*.

EM: It's been a long time.

RM: So you remember, sort of.

EM: Yes. Yeah.

RM: Good. But even if you just thought I was a stranger, do you think I'm a likable enough person?

EM: Right. That's true.

RM: So we could have a conversation even if you forgot my name.

EM: I don't know.

RM: Probably?

EM: I'd have to say I don't know.

RM: So you're just being polite? You're just agreeing with me?

EM: Mmm hmm.

RM: Okay?

EM: *Okay.*

RM: 'Cause I love you, and I've known you for over 50 years, y'know?

EM: I love *you.*

RM: That's wonderful. And we've known each other half a century.

EM: A long time.

RM: As long as I've been around, I've been your son and you've been my mom. *Mom.* (I kiss her forehead.)

EM: Wonderful.

RM: Is it time for *Wheel of Fortune?*

EM: It is. It's right now.

RM: Or *Jeopardy?*

EM: Yes. *Jeopardy* comes first.

WHEN J.D. WAS IN FLOWER

For years, I was puzzled by the confluence of two events in the fall of '57: my mother's first home dye job and her throwing in the towel as a teacher. They happened within weeks of each other.

Before starting the new year at Andrew Jackson H.S., to cover the grey, she dyed herself flaming red with an off-brand of storebought slop—first time she was ever anything but a dark brunette. It looked pretty fake, and kind of tawdry—the way a lot of rock-roll chicks *try* to look these days—conspicuously painted. I was a little embarrassed for her.

A couple weeks later, she came home one day and announced she'd had enough. It made no sense. Her claim that "Teaching isn't for me anymore" didn't play at all. No warning, no buildup . . . too abrupt. She was only 41.

It would be 25 years before I would learn the uh Truth behind the concurrence, when finally my father, with supreme sarcasm, spilled it for me:

A remedial math class—she hated those—always a buncha rowdies. During a lull in the proceedings, a "juvenile delinquent" (or maybe just a clown) yelled from the back of the room: "Hey, Mrs. Meltzer, stand on your head so we can see if you're a natural redhead." (Rock and fucking ROLL!)

She walked out and quit on the spot.

The thing with my mom is that, for all her dress-up and flaunt, she never had the slightest sense of just how much sexual heat she INVOLUNTARILY emitted (as opposed to *exhibited* . . . or *felt* down in her cells), or if she had a sense, a glimmering, it made her hopelessly squeamish. She didn't understand her basic ALLURE, she just couldn't handle it.

And to suddenly have this scuzzy lout draw loud attention to her PUSSY! . . . poor mommy!

GOO-GOO GA-GA

And I even slept with her once, um, *at least* once, maybe more. I vividly remember one time—I was maybe 10.

The old man was gone—his only overnighter during my childhood. His gloomy father was getting his cataracts plucked, and his mother, a frantic old ninny, wanted him there. Which made for some very weird energy in the house—neither unpleasant nor pleasant, just weird. Anyway, I got lucky.

I lay in bed listening to the sounds of TV, then TV was done and I still wasn't sleeping, and my windup clock ticked louder and louder, and it got later, much later, than I'd ever been awake. I couldn't sleep and I couldn't sleep and at some point I think I might actually have been groaning, and my mother let me come in and sleep with her.

Oh baby! What a sweet-ain't-the-*word* occurrence: real goo-goo ga-ga time. She didn't snuggle or cuddle or offer me a shoulder or an arm to rest my mournful little head on, or offer anything, really, with a physical dimension, but hey, c'mon . . . you can't have everything.

You've gotta figure, in the same way that she never nursed me, she prob'ly just put me in a crib as soon as we both got back from the hospital, from birthing, so it's possible, even probable, this was the ONLY time I slept with her—there's nobody alive to tell it diff'rent.

Look—I'm not one of those once-is-not-enough type guys, give-'em-an-inch-they-want-a-foot . . . malcontents, y'know? Once with this dame was plenty sufficient . . . yes YES! I wouldn't shit ya.

HEAVEN

At 2 AM (2003), I toss and sweat and try to catch a thread of anything that might help me remember the Fonz's real name—who played him—and the show John Travolta was on . . . this is really troubling me. Even on a piecemeal basis, keeping up the pretense of total cultural recall—40 percent of my writerly *shtick*—can be a tough row to hoe.

And while I'm struggling with this horseshit, hours before the answers come to me, a verrrry distant memory sidles into my consciousness: that my mother actually SANG for me, oh, two-three-four times, probably on consecutive days, to settle me into my afternoon nap. The song each time was "My Blue Heaven."

Just Molly and me, and baby makes three. With my baby sister, we were already four, so I didn't take it literally, but gosh

GOLLY—could THIS have been my mother's perception of our life/lived? Was the Meltzer House of Dysfunction really a "little nest"? Her voice was more grating than soothing, the notes were off, but she didn't stumble over the words, and the overall experience was *way* more agreeable than not. On first listen, I misheard *Molly* as *Mommy*.

Or is most—or all—of this simply how I'm *choosing* to remember things—to reel in and stack the shards of a hypothetical (and barely even anecdotal) yesterday? Is my mommy-lore remembrance quotient worth its weight in slugpiss?

Really, what was I thinking when I said she had no interest in music? Or was "My Blue Heaven" where it all came to a screeching halt?

Wish I knew *whose* version she learned it from . . . certainly not Fats Domino's.

OH MAMA
(CAN THIS REALLY BE THE END?)

I always imagined that someday I would get to hold the mothermom "accountable." Not in a scales-of-justice sort of way where I would dangle evidence of ill will or errant causality or any such shuck, but simply . . . well . . . I assumed I would get a chance to talk the past over with her—talk it *pointedly*.

Fat chance now.

Before my father lost his ability to hold a pencil or concentrate on anything for more than a minute, I encouraged him, for really no reason but to get his engine spinning, to write to me about his beginnings—his primal memories. He sent me maybe 10, 15 illegible rambles about his parents, his sister, life in Brooklyn in the 1920s, and from a later period, what he thought of FDR—stories I'd probably heard 100 times before. In the course of his letters he kept repeating the same stories, in the very same words . . . like a tape replay. After he could no longer write, I had him tape me his rememb'rings . . . and those too kept coming up identical.

Anyway, I was sure I would eventually get my mom to take a verbal walk through some of *her* old sights and scenes.

Too late for that one too.

It was less than ten years ago that I found out her father had killed himself when I was two. The line had always been that he died of a heart attack. Talking to some cousin or somebody, my sister discovered otherwise, and my mother conceded, "*Oh* yes"—very matter-o-factly—"he took his own life." (Who knows how many secrets of hers have by now become defunct secrets? Forgotten concealments in lapsed databases, they're not anything anymore, not even lint . . . they're simply *not*.)

The only time she and I came anywhere near discussing the concept of death was on the phone when Artie's wife died in the early '90s. "You sound depressed," I told her.

"Well, it makes you think . . . "

"About your own mortality?"

". . . . . . Yeah."

End of conversation.

Whatever it is that life "means," I've never been able to convey to this woman especially much of what it means to *me*, to dialogue it with her in any significant way. Not when she was totally with it . . . and now I daren't even try.

Some years ago, when I read her a snippet of a poem I'd written, a riff on the theme of there not being enough total love in the universe to fill the heart of ONE lonely man, she shrugged it off with a *heh heh heh*. Now, I'm guessing—and all I *can* do is guess—it would sadden her as even just a mock-up notion, a cosmic disclaimer, a moment's toss-off not wedded or welded to my being or hers or to anyone else's. Why fucking sadden her, 'specially when she appears, for broad twinklings at least, to be a functional (if preposterous) approximation of "happy"?

Likewise, there are "insights" I wish I'd been able to score off of HER in the course of this life-strut we've chacha'ed. One thing I've never had a clue about—emotional, intellectual, whatever—is this wacked-out business of Blood Relation. When my father was still alive, and all four partners in the Meltzer Experiment would get together after longtimes apart, about an hour into things I'd corner my sister and ask her what she thought the blood thing was about . . . 'cuz even staring it in the face, I couldn't figure it. Later on, when I'd try and prod the matriarch of our club into oozing a little of her own take on the matter, it was always just more of the *heh heh* . . . keep it.

It occurs to me that families have permanent legitimacy mainly to their begetters: parents. The begotten grow up and scram, their connection to the club shifts and mutates like crazy fug-all, but parents are maintainers of the glue, and in spite of all else, long as they retain their wits, their willingness, they remain gluemasters.

And when the wits are gone and the glue (qua glue) is gone, well, it's just about people, with all their relational baggage, decades apart in age, galaxies apart in experience, relating to each other as, well, people. Nothing is ever neutral or symmetrical, or anything like reciprocal—everyone's baggage is immense, and too immensely complicated—but maybe if you're fortunate you can wing a sort of neutral non-neutrality . . . a less baggaged baggagedness. Or is this just some sappy, genteel commonplace I for too many reasons never clenched my teeth on before? Dunno.

Aside from the mem probs (and the node false alarm), my mother seems as healthy as the proverbial horse. She takes quarter-mile walks (supervised, of course). At 80, she still played tennis. I've always felt that if she didn't make it to 90, she was being cheated. Well, she *will* make it to 90, but who and what will "she" be by then, as her conscious mind skates closer, ever closer, to non-ness?

My father was almost dust before he stopped being a world-class asshole. My mother isn't an asshole, she never was an asshole, but who/what she is still very much escapes me. As her bare feet start straddling the Pit, and I look yonder to a time when she ISN'T, I suspect that a true sense of her being, her non-non-ness, will if anything, by then, have escaped me by an even greater margin.

MILK OF MAGNESIA

This morning I was on a checkout line at the supermarket when this woman sez to me: "Milk of magnesia???"

"What?" She was Filipino, wearing a nurse outfit, and her eyes were on my forearm.

"Why you tattoo milk of magnesia?"

"Huh?"

"M.O.M."

Hospital code for a laxative. How neat!

SHANGRI-LA

1937. Esther Bersin, 21, and three girlfriends step outside the Strand Theater, Far Rockaway, N.Y. They take bracing gulps of night air and walk past the bus stop from which they planned, originally, to ride back to their homes in Rockaway Beach.

They've just seen Frank Capra's *Lost Horizon*, a movie Esther will talk about for at least the next 30 years, and are all so blown away by its rendering of Hollywood utopia in the snowy Himalayas, not to mention its vision of a Better World, that they continue to walk, as if on a cloud, blissfully smiling, saying not a word. Though they each live between three and four miles away, and pass any number of stops en route, the thought of taking a bus doesn't occur to them.

My mom the utopian . . .

Long into her tenure as Esther Meltzer, *Lost Horizon* will loom large in her synopto-whatsosphere. Its male and female leads will keep playing crucial roles in her life, foxtrotting her all the way to middle age. Ronald Colman's sole TV vehicle, *The Halls of Ivy* (CBS, Tues., 8:30–9:00), a show even TIME will in short order forget, will end up as her top show of the 1950s, while the benign presence of Jane Wyatt on *Father Knows Best* will make that show required nuke-family viewing, despite its limited viability to the rest of the household.

By the time the movie itself is televised, enabling her to share it, at long last, with the whole damn family, a jack-a-dandy suave and handsome as Colman himself will occupy the White House—a dandy whose own better-world song-&-dance will feel my-t-viable to her adolescent son . . . making him easy prey for utopian hi-jinx on a snowy-blowy soundstage.

It's a life!

DICKIE

Sitting tall in my saddle as I survey the attrition, the dissolution, the termination in the most strictly self-centered of ways, I can't help but reflect upon one perk in the deal above all others: that while I still know this person, this woman, this rare bird as the former Mommy, she hasn't an atom of an inkling of me as the former Dickie.

There are myriad things that either or both of us ain't no more, but here and now, on this last merry roundup, those two—and in particular, the latter—will more than do.

As sole caretaker of the shenanigan, I say *Begone!!*

From this minute forth, all azure dawns of my peeny will be LOWERCASE, not upper.

(What the bloody hey.)

METAL

Red snapper is the lettuce of
fish.

Strawberry is an expecially
scaly fish among fruit.

You know you're nearer the
End when all these
bits 'n'
flecks
scraps
trash
stick to your feet.

A STIFF FOR ALL SEASONS

We were never anything like friends. I was in the same room, space or vicinity as Charles Bukowski, who on August 16th would have been 77, five-six-seven times, total.

The first of those times, in the spring of '72, somewhere in the hills up near Griffith Park, he was carrying a jug of red table wine and a bag of groceries, dinner-plus for himself and the woman he was then seeing, the publicity director of a record company that had flown me to L.A. to write a feature on a weepy-sensitive singer/songwriter. The first thing I heard him say, handing her the groceries, opening the wine, was "Lucy, tonight I'm gonna bite off your ugly white insect of a clit."

I could say now that I was impressed, a wide-eyed, slave-to-my-gonads writeboy hearing it done "for real" (in "real time") by a veteran gonad-slave poet, but I wasn't; or that I thought he was a fuckhead, which I did, but I thought then that most people were fuckheads. What I thought was *Gee, how premeditated.* He'd obviously been saving and savoring the line all day. (The only other person I'd met who spoke in headlines and captions was Patti Smith.)

I hadn't read a word by the man at the time, but in retrospect I can see it was all there—a goldmine of lit-crit etcetera: the bombastic second-person hostility; master use of the unvarnished raw; the moment's utterance crystallized in lucite forever; the merger of sublime (image, structure, intent) and sordid; the here-I-come-I'm-Bukowski (to the tune of "Hey, hey, we're the Monkees") leitmotif and business card; the downscale populism (not everyone a king/queen but every person—especially those in "relationships"—a chump); the inseparable themes of pleasure-in-anguish, anguish-in-pleasure; the highly mannered, if "simplified," caste/gender/class rituals; the (perhaps ingenuous) lead-with-your-chin insistence on trouble; the live-as-you-write/write-as-you-live chalkboard pep talk (with chalk strokes a-grating); the matchless clarity of spew.

All there for sure, but mostly I thought, *What a silly old man.* Later that night, after we'd finished the wine and gone on to beer, he announced: "Now I'm gonna watch TV on purpose for the first time." He'd been in the same room with it on, he said, but never really paid attention. Lucy had a brand new many-inch Panasonic.

First thing on was an episode of *Cannon* with William Conrad undercover as a trucker. When the ol' tubbo showed some mettle in subduing a runaway 18-wheeler, Bukowski poured on the sarcasm: "What a man!" At hour's end, after fatty blew his second shot at a frowsy old flame: "You're better off without her!" Next up, talk-show beast George Putnam, whom Buk let really have it: "Go ahead—pick on the poor goddam Commies!" Around 1:00 or 2:00, when the film started skipping on *I Shot Jesse James* with John Ireland (was the projectionist asleep?): "See!—they haven't got the technology down *yet*." A funny old blustery guy. He reminded me of my white-haired grandmother talking to and at the family's first TV in 1950, but more blustery. Four years later I went to the fights with him.

*   *   *

If you felt like it, it wouldn't be too big a cheat to divide Bukowski's published works into three basic categories: poems, novels, short stories. I mean *anybody's* writing could be split that way—big deal—anybody with substantial stacks of each, but with Mr. B the distinctions were matters of more than formal deviation. Different types of work meant vastly different ways of working.

The poems were essentially all written in one sitting, a few at a time—day, night—whatever. A verbatim record of what he was then and there thinking, beer at his side, pecking away. At the opposite end are the novels, representing commitment to the long haul, willful acts of episodic fiction over several months at least (with life as ongoingly lived filtered out, kept at bay, not directly intruding). The stories, requiring multiple (or at least prolonged) sittings, fall between quick fix and long haul, closer to the former in narrative scale and duration (usually a single experience), to the latter in compositional fuss and import. Neither fish nor fowl, they tend to be the glibbest of his outings, though never as glib as—and always more real, more alive, than—the stories of Raymond Carver, f'rinstance.

The poems, at best, are the high point of his art. At worst (and a lot, prob'ly even most, of his published verse is chuck-off and filler), they're still never as bad, never make you wince a tenth as much, as the average off poem by a John Ashberry, a John Berryman, a Stephen Spender. If anything, they're a deconstruction of all that, never aspiring to heights of "poetic" ado, never stretching for metaphoric interlock, never burdening sight lines with the slop of transcendence or arcania or even wit for wit sake. Or if not never, almost.

Bukowski the poet speaks quite like a normal human being, or a normal ornery old cuss with a standard vocabulary and an axe to grind. His poetic scribblings read easy, which is to say they read like prose, because virtually they are—prose with a high count of white space, a minimum of fat. (The opposite of Kerouac, whose most poetic moments are in his designated prose, Bukowski's finest prose is in his poems.) This is poetry at its least impregnable, about which Todd Grimson once wrote: "He says things that are actually not that easy to say, in speech or in print, but especially in print—it's not the tradition. But once said, because it all *reads* so easy, it's as though they've always been said—they smell universal."

*   *   *

The Ring Record Book says 8/7/76, so that's the date it was: Danny "Little Red" Lopez vs. Art Hafey, L.A. Forum. Elimination match for the WBC featherweight title. Winner gets a shot at champion David "Poison" Kotey in Ghana. I had a couple tickets, so I called Bukowski. Sure, why not, it's free, I'm driving, he'll go.

At his place on Carlton Way in Hollywood I got to see the "setup." How the Great Writer writes. In his typewriter, an old black manual, sat an unfinished page, prose, single-spaced. "Not double? There's no room for corrections." "No corrections! What I write is *perfect*." On the floor beside his desk were many days'/nights' worth of empty Budweiser bottles; on the wall, a huge active spider web. When I tried to read the perfect prose, he handed me a scrapbook.

Page after page of woman photos, many of them captioned. "You get older, you think it might get easier, it doesn't. The hangovers get tougher, the heartache gets tougher." He shows me a recent entry, a posed pic of a leggy blond, younger than me, with the inscription "Whoa, sailor!" "She tore my *guts* out." A brief pause. "They all do."

In the car I unbag the six-pack I bought for the occasion, hand him a Lucky Lager. "Lucky?! What piss." He tilts the bottle at an outlandish angle, more vertical than Dizzy Gillespie's custom-bent trumpet, downs half of it. "The things they tell you. Shit. She had a pussy the size of this window, and she thinks I'll . . ." Leaning out, he fails to complete the thought. "Whudda you think of James M. Cain?" I ask, apropos of everything and nothing. "Cain? Listen, kid, you should be reading Dostoevski. Knut Hamsun. At least Céline." He finishes his Lucky, slams it behind the seat—smash. I hand him another.

During prelims, this gruff muh-fuh showed a decided compassion for losers—"C'mon ref, stop it, the kid's helpless"—very touching, actually. When I noted there were no heavyweights on the bill, nobody in fact above welterweight,

he grumbled, "Heavyweights are just big salamis," a character-
ization I'll never forget. Before the main event had started,
many beers were consumed by us both.

Against Canadian journeyman Hafey, the on-again/off-
again Lopez had the advantage in height, reach, punch,
aggressiveness and savvy. And, though it really wasn't tested,
heart as well. Hafey showed none. All he did was stand up and
get pounded round after round, never penetrating Lopez's
range, never really trying. "C'mon, Hafey," bellowed
Bukowksi, "make believe he's your mother-in-law." The advice
unheeded, Hafey was TKO'ed in 7. "Boxing is the last bastion
of courage," sighed his advisor. You bet.

*   *   *

gunned down outside the Seaside Motel I stand looki
ng at the live lobster in a fishshop on the Redondo
Beach pier the redhead gone to torture other males
it's raining again it's raining again and again som
etimes I think of Bogart and I don't like Bogart an
y more kuv stuff mox out—when you get a little mon
ey in the bank you can write down anything on the p
age call it Art and pull the chain gunned down in a
fishmarket the lobsters you see they get caught lik
e we get caught.

—"Kuv Stuff Mox Out" (excerpt)

Many drunks have written and many have written drunk
and many, drunk, have written from and about their drinking
or tried to (*you* try it: 's harder'n hell), but few, ever, have

pulled off the likes of Bukowski's "Kuv Stuff Mox Out"—hey. His greatest single work? A *classic*. Not the reconstituted/ reconditioned meat and "psychophysics" of the drunk state, of a night's drinking, but a sharp-eyed/dull-eyed/no-eyed blank-slate transcript of the bleary details, *during*, present tense, real time, real *writer's* time, at the typewriter: write, don't stop, fill page—reach right margin, carriage return, no hyphen—continue until you lose consciousness or interest. From before he had a machine with auto-return . . .

* * *

And yet *Barfly*, shit.

If at the time of its release in book form you considered the screenplay to *Barfly*, the film before which Bukowski was STILL a well-kept secret in his own town, his own country, a novel, which in page count and chronology it kind of is, it would probably have rated no higher than his worst or second worst (either better than *Factotum*—slightly—or not even). Three days or whatever in the life of a neighborhood bar— wheel out the clichés . . . flog 'em till they drop . . . draw outlines, heavy outlines, 'round everything and everybody . . . replace effortless natural with ponderous fake . . . see Spot puke. Better than *Days of Wine and Roses*, certainly "darker" than *Cheers*, but what wasn't?

Hey. Chances are good—likely—certain—Kerouac will inevitably be known to the gen'ral public as a cardboard lobby card to the spuzzpuff film made from *On the Road*, only he's long dead, there's not much he can do about it. Bukowski was not only alive for *Barfly*, he wrote the damn thing. And not only did he write it, given all latitude and encouragement to create anything he fucking wanted, HE had final cut on the script as shot . . . fuggit.

* * *

> a woman told a man
> when he got off a plane
> that I was dead.
> a magazine printed
> the fact that I was dead
> and somebody else said
> that they'd heard that I
> was dead, and then somebody
> wrote an article and said
> our Rimbaud our Villon is
> dead. at the same time an old
> drinking buddy published
> a piece stating that I
> could no longer write. a
> real Judas job. they can't
> wait for me to go, these
> farts.
>
> —"Up Your Yellow River"

A repetitive guy, this Bukowski, but one theme he really took to task—pushed to the limit—fuck the limit—was death. Mortality. His own in tandem with others', everyone's, but especially his own—the death of his ass—and the loss of his handle on writing. So often did he rehearse this biz that by the actual end, shoot, years and *years* before the end, it read like a celebration of sorts, a tacky (and increasingly hollow) before-the-fact commemoration. As meat for major text, for the unit poem even, he'd pretty much used it up.

(One thing you don't find much of in his late poems is present-tense relational anguish—current reference to anyone tearing his guts out. After years of women as "collaborators" in his art, suddenly they're absent from any reasonably ferocious foreground play. As retold ancient history, sure, there's still enough of that stuff, but nothing with Linda, his 20-years-younger second wife, as sourcepoint. He writes not insulting-ly of her affection for Meher Baba, speaks of turning down the radio—no problem—'cause she's having her period. Talks pleasantly about buying her a car. Is it credible that, domesti-cally at least, he'd become less of a crank/cuss/sonofabitch? "Serenity" had somehow kicked in? Or/and he simply chose not to alienate the one person he trusted to stick around for his last syllable of supported time? Dunno; dunno; dunno.)

When he finally croaked in March of '94, of leukemia or some such, the front-page obit in the *L.A. Times* read: "Charles Bukowski Dies; Poet of L.A.'s Low-Life." Do some-thing like *Barfly*—and "go Hollywood"—what can you expect? And the Hollywood rap is not, ahem, ill-taken. Might've been if he hadn't followed the movie with a novel about its making, *Hollywood*, easily his breeziest, most trifling, least *interesting* big hunka fiction. An exasperatingly typical piece of tinseltown fluff. (Apprentice writers from Squodunk have come closer to "nailing" the subject.) Hang out with Sean Penn and Madonna, fine, but this book was sad to see.

After he was dead a couple minutes, his final novel, *Pulp*, was issued. In it, he encounters Lady Death, who hires him to find a not-yet-dead Louis-Ferdinand Céline. She's a good broad, though, and when it gets to be *his* turn he can almost dig it. Must've known he was dying when he wrote it, and the last sentence ends: "and the blaze and the blare of yellow swept over and enveloped me." That's nice, I like it—yellow is my favorite color.

* * *

So while I'm working on this piece—life is funny—I find myself in one of his poems. "The Jackals," in *The Last Night of the Earth Poems*, p. 312—you could look it up. Nobody leaves him alone—he wrote lots of *those*—and in this one three people won't leave him alone, and I'm one of them. Doesn't name me but it's me. Written somewhere in the late '80s.

I was at a screening of some videos he did for French TV with the director of *Barfly*, Barbet Schroeder. Little three-minute bursts, talking, reading, arguing with Linda, good stuff actually. Before they ran 'em Bukowski and I got in a conversation. And really, it *was* a conversation, back and forth, the closest I ever came to normal blah blah with the guy—till suddenly he decided he'd had enough and he growled at me, "Give me air to breathe," and walked away. Fair enough.

So he goes home, how long could he have waited to put it down, the dialogue, a day, two days, a week?—and how could he, the master of verbatim, the quick fixer, get it wrong?—but he gets it wrong. The words spoken. First of all, it's not "air to breathe"—good line—but "get the fuck away from me" (how trite). Then he has me pitch for a shitty mag I was then writing for—*Spin*—claiming I said, "it's going to be better than *Rolling Stone*," which I would *never* have said, ha, like *Golf Digest* is better than *Rolling Stone*, *Pacific Beach Pennysaver* is better than *Rolling Stone*, anything is better than *Rolling Stone*, but *Spin*, then as now, was no bargain. What I said was this young fool, the trendy foppish son of Bob Guccione, had a terrible mag that was paying good money, and he wanted me to interview the Great Poet, but only if the Great Poet would also interview me—a thousand bucks apiece, just let the tape run—to which he said, "Sounds good to me."

That was only a small piece of the encounter. He remembered me without my having to say (as misquoted), "remember me?"—he looked at me, thought for a sec and said, "Lucy, right?," then asked about Lucy. She was kind of down and out, I told him, in a halfway house in New York for manic-depressives. "That's too bad," he said, "she was one of the *good ones*." "After you dumped her," I told him, "she said, 'I wouldn't give him the ice in winter.'" "That's a great line! I'm gonna use it." He remembered Art Hafey.

In his poem he gets pissed about my write-up of our trip to the fights. Says I'd "attacked" him. Mostly I just quoted him—affectionately—as he jabbered away, and he *did* jabber, I'm sure we both jabbered. When I showed him the piece at the time, he only complained that I was confusing boxing and horse racing ("Keep it up, kid—eventually you'll get it right"), but that's okay, you remember old b.s. the way you wanna remember it.

There's more he gets wrong from the night of the screening, including the letter I then sent (telling him in all humility, all sincerity, that I thought of him as a brother), but that doesn't bother me, nor my being a prop for his obsession with privacy (all exhibitionists require it), a hair-trigger for his paranoia and self-loathing. What bothers me is his fucking up the verbatim. Missing—avoiding—the true specificity.

So the poems are not only prose, gosh, they're FICTION. Well I'll be dipped—sorry I'm such a simp—but *that* feels like a letdown.

And I can't find, now that I've read everything, any use ANYWHERE of "ice in winter."

*   *   *

IN THE END, let Bukowski be this: a means, a standard, for measuring our own orneriness, our trashy fatality, our fuckdance with our own weary detritus, our big stink. What writer, in any end, could covet, crave or fancy more than that?

HOME

Spill not my ashes
in the Ganges, babe.
Scatter them
to the stinging
wind
on raindark streets
of your own choosing,
but reserve a table-
spoon or two
for the groove
of your filthy fat
butt.
Rub some of me there
with your little
fingers,
deep and
dirty—
would ya do
that, darlin'?